Strength lies in differences, not in similarities.

—Stephen Covey

Love's a Mystery

Love's a Mystery in Sleepy Hollow, New York
Love's a Mystery in Cape Disappointment, Washington
Love's a Mystery in Cut and Shoot, Texas
Love's a Mystery in Nameless, Tennessee
Love's a Mystery in Hazardville, Connecticut
Love's a Mystery in Deadwood, Oregon
Love's a Mystery in Gnaw Bone, Indiana
Love's a Mystery in Tombstone, Arizona
Love's a Mystery in Peculiar, Missouri

Love's a Mystery

in

Peculiar
MO

Emily Quinn
& Laura Bradford

Guideposts

Love's a Mystery is a trademark of Guideposts.

Published by Guideposts Books & Inspirational Media
100 Reserve Road, Suite E200
Danbury, CT 06810
Guideposts.org

Copyright © 2023 by Guideposts. All rights reserved.

This book, or parts thereof, may not be reproduced, stored in a retrieval system, or transmitted in any form or by any means, electronic, mechanical, photocopying, recording, or otherwise, without the written permission of the publisher.

This is a work of fiction. While the setting of Love's a Mystery as presented in this series is fictional, the locations actually exist, and some places and characters may be based on actual places and people whose identities have been used with permission or fictionalized to protect their privacy. Apart from the actual people, events, and locales that figure into the fiction narrative, all other names, characters, businesses, and events are the creation of the author's imagination and any resemblance to actual persons or events is coincidental.

Every attempt has been made to credit the sources of copyrighted material used in this book. If any such acknowledgment has been inadvertently omitted or miscredited, receipt of such information would be appreciated.

Scripture references are from the following sources: *The Holy Bible, King James Version* (KJV). *The Holy Bible, New International Version* (NIV). Copyright ©1973, 1978, 1984, 2011 by Biblica, Inc. Used by permission of Zondervan. All rights reserved worldwide. www.zondervan.com.

Cover and interior design by Müllerhaus.
Cover illustration by Dan Burr at Illustration Online LLC.
Typeset by Aptara, Inc.

Printed and bound in the United States of America
10 9 8 7 6 5 4 3 2 1

Love is Growing

by
Emily Quinn

Why fit in when you were born to stand out?

—Dr. Seuss

Chapter One

Baltimore, Maryland
1960

Rhoda Grey studied herself in the mirror. The new bright orange and green dress she'd bought over the weekend felt too short for work. Or maybe her legs were just too long. Either way, the outfit wasn't modest enough for her job at the insurance office.

She sat on the bed and checked the length again. No matter what the salesgirl had told her, there was no way she could pull this off. She wanted to look more like the women she saw on television. Like Mrs. Kennedy as she campaigned for her husband. The only problem was, Rhoda hated hats and couldn't afford designer clothes. She'd gone with something the salesclerk had assured her everyone was wearing. She carefully took the dress off and put it back on the hanger. She'd have to return it after work tomorrow. She didn't know what she'd buy to replace it. All the dresses seemed to be more in tune with being a fun young chick going to a concert rather than the office.

Rhoda was definitely not a chick. No matter what the vernacular of the day wanted to call her.

Rhoda hurried and dressed in her standard Monday outfit and bypassed the mirror. She knew how she looked. Drab, old, and grey, just like her name. No wonder she was passed over for promotion.

No one could see her. Although how she was overlooked when she towered over every other woman on her floor, she didn't know.

Rhoda grabbed her coat and purse. Before heading to work, she wanted to run upstairs to the rooftop and check on her tomato plants. There were a few minutes before she had to catch her bus. The warm weather and mild temperatures for the last few days had helped the seedlings, but she still worried about a frost in these early days of May. She'd grown the plants from seeds, and they were still tiny. Their size was an advantage if it did freeze. It kept them close to the ground and out of the worst of the night air.

She quickly locked her door and took the stairs to the roof. Her apartment was on the fifth floor, so it didn't take long. The five pots were lined up on the edge of the roof, sheltered by a brick wall that heated up during the day and gave the plants warmth long after the sun had set. She touched a leaf, her thoughts going to her childhood home, where she'd helped her mother plant the garden every spring.

Now that house was gone, having been sold to pay for the funeral costs after the accident that killed her parents. She was alone in the world and, because of that, she needed to get to work. The only person she could count on was herself.

The moon slipped out of view as the sun rose. Presidential candidates were talking about sending a man to the moon. It looked like a long, lonely trip. She liked being on the ground. Even being up on the rooftop, a good place for the plants to get consistent sunlight, was too high for Rhoda. She felt connected to the earth, or she had when she'd gardened with her mother. The memory was so long ago now, her grasp on it was fleeting. She said a quick goodbye to the plants and hurried downstairs.

Once on the bus, she watched as they navigated different neighborhoods, gathering people from all walks of life. Caucasian, Hispanic, African American, a person's background didn't matter on the bus. It was truly the melting pot she'd learned about in school. Everyone just waited to start their workday. Some people chatted about their families and events they were going to, but she didn't have anyone to talk with. She nodded to the woman who'd sat down next to her. "Good morning. Happy Monday."

The woman grunted and then leaned back and closed her eyes.

Not interested in conversation, then. Rhoda turned to the window and to watching the world go by outside the bus. She always tried, but she never seemed to find someone willing to share their thoughts with her, not even for the few minutes they were stuck in the same vehicle.

So, instead, she planned out her next row of plants. The building manager didn't mind her using the rooftop as long as she took care of them and didn't let them die and look bad. Clarence was very concerned about how the public areas of the building looked, which she appreciated. It was nice coming home to a clean entryway. A lot of the buildings around her didn't look as friendly or inviting. Maybe later this summer she'd ask if she could plant flowers on the outside step. There were two empty planter boxes that Clarence never filled with life. Daisies would be nice against the red brick. Or purple petunias.

She realized that her stop was next, and she stood as they approached the corner. The driver glanced back, caught her movement, and called out the street corner. The woman who'd been sitting next to her was already gone. She must have left during Rhoda's musing about flowers.

The city was preparing for the political rally that was being held that weekend. Street sweepers cleaned the debris from the streets, and landscapers hung baskets on the streetlights. The city looked pretty, like what she imagined a small town might look like. Adding plants to downtown Baltimore's concrete and steel made it feel more approachable. She might stay around to maybe catch a glimpse of the senator who was now running for president. The news said he was drop-dead gorgeous. Of course, that one factor wasn't enough to win Rhoda's vote in November.

The noise of the city hit her as soon as she stepped off the bus and onto the sidewalk. Horns honked, vehicles drove past, and the doors on the bus slammed shut behind her as it took off for its next stop. She weaved through people on the sidewalk and finally reached the doors to her office building. When she stepped inside the foyer, the line to the elevator almost reached the door. Instead of waiting there, she punched in at the time clock and then headed to the stairs to start her day.

At her desk, she tucked her purse into her drawer, hung up her coat on a hook in her cubicle, and then opened the first file in her inbox. She had two boxes. One was labeled *in*, the other *out*. Her new supervisor, April, came in earlier than the clerks to drop off the day's work on each desk. At random times during the day she'd come back and retrieve the files from Rhoda's outbox. Rhoda always had more in her inbox at the beginning of the day than the other clerks. Yet, when the supervisor slot had opened, she hadn't even been interviewed for the position. She'd gotten a form letter thanking her for her interest and informing her that a more qualified candidate had been chosen.

She knew April hadn't been the top producer, but she did possess one skill Rhoda didn't. She talked a lot. To everyone. Rhoda couldn't even imagine chatting with each person on the floor, including the bosses as they came by. How would she get any work done?

At ten, April came to Rhoda's desk and picked up the completed files. "You've done a lot of work this morning, Rhoda. I'm so lucky to have you in my group." She lowered her voice. "Mr. Henry would like to see you." She gestured to the boss's office as if Rhoda didn't know where it was located.

Rhoda stood and ran her hands down the cotton dress she'd put on that morning. Now she was glad she hadn't taken the chance on the orange one, but she wished she had something newer on. She pushed her hair off her shoulders. "Do you know what he wants to talk about?"

April shook her head. "I asked, but he said it was personal and I was to go get you. If he wants to know if I'm doing a good job, please say yes. I really need to keep this position."

For a minute, Rhoda really saw the woman behind the mask April put on every day. She was just as nervous about this meeting as Rhoda was, especially if it was an evaluation of the new supervisor's abilities. She smiled at April. "You're doing a great job."

April blinked and then smiled back. "Thank you. I thought, well, I assumed, you would be the one they promoted. You're so good at all this."

Yes, I'd thought that as well. Rhoda hoped the opinion didn't show on her face. "Thank you for saying that. I better get going and see what Mr. Henry wants."

"Oh yes, of course." April moved away, letting Rhoda step out of her cubicle toward the line of offices by the windows.

She knocked on Mr. Henry's door and stepped inside when she heard his response.

"Miss Grey, I'd like to introduce you to Mr. Reynolds. He's our corporate attorney and would like to speak with you." Mr. Henry made the introduction to the man standing next to him and then, to Rhoda's surprise, stepped toward the door. He paused before exiting the room. "Take as long as you need. I'll be getting some coffee."

Mr. Reynolds pointed to the visitor chair then moved to sit behind Mr. Henry's desk. "This won't take long. I've received correspondence from an attorney in Missouri. Apparently, this Jacob Stine didn't have your home address, so his office reached out to the company, asking if I'd be the intermediary in this matter."

Rhoda sat in the chair she'd been directed to. "I'm sorry, Mr. Reynolds, exactly what matter are you handling?"

"You've been named as a beneficiary in a will. A Mr. Frederick James left you a farm and some belongings in a small town in Missouri. It's near the Kansas border." He passed her a file folder as he studied her. "Here are the documents. I'm sure Mr. Henry would approve some leave for you to go there and settle the estate. You may come back with some money to buy a whole new wardrobe."

"I looked for a new dress this weekend, but it's hard…" Rhoda stopped talking. Mr. Reynolds wasn't really interested in her clothes. Likely he'd said that because he thought all young women her age were interested only in the latest fashions. "Anyway, I don't understand. I inherited a farm?"

"Just what a young career girl in Baltimore needs, right?" He stood and held out his hand. "Congratulations. There's a list of people you need to contact. If you don't want to go across the country to settle this, I've been told that there are several offers to purchase the land. You could do most of it from here. The lawyer in Missouri will explain all that when you call."

"Thank you for letting me know." She shook his hand and clutched at the envelope he'd given her with the other.

"Be sure to keep Mr. Henry informed of your plans. I hear you're a valuable part of his team." The look he gave her as he walked out of the office showed he didn't believe that anyone who looked like her could be a valuable part of any team.

She took a deep breath and read the will. When she finished, she leaned back, shocked. What was she going to do with a farm in Missouri? In a town named Peculiar, no less.

Peculiar, Missouri

Martin Oaks paused in front of the large red barn that held the new tractor and equipment he'd brought home from Kansas City last month. He'd be the first farmer in the area to use the modern technology. A fact his father never failed to remind him of at the dinner table when he went up to the main house to eat fried chicken and mashed potatoes with his parents after church. Martin knew he was doing the right thing. Now he needed the crop yields to increase so he could replenish his savings that he'd just depleted when he wrote that check.

He leaned over and rubbed Bo's head. The black Labrador retriever had been his constant companion since his tenth birthday—the age his dad had felt he was old enough to take care of another life. Now his dad had retired from running Oaks Farm and was enjoying his golden years with Mom. He hung around Peculiar and had breakfast with the old guys at the diner in town. A lot of conversation at that table probably centered on Martin's newfangled notions about running a farm, but Martin didn't care. Much.

He'd been invited to visit the KS Seed Company in a week. They were sponsoring a class on innovations in farming. The costs of the travel were on his dime, but they were putting the class attendees up in a hotel and feeding them. He assumed they wanted his seed order this year, and he'd more than likely give it to them, even without the perks. But if there was something new he needed to think about, he was willing to give them the time.

"Your dad was in Sally's this morning with his cronies when I stopped to get some breakfast with my brother." Nate Jones walked up and gave Bo a quick rub on the head. "He asked what crazy notions we implemented this week on the farm. He really doesn't like your methods, does he?"

Martin chuckled at his farm manager's question. He hadn't heard Nate walk up behind him. He'd been lost in his daydreams. "Dad thinks if it's not broke, don't fix it. But if we don't do something, we're going to be priced out of the market. If we can even keep enough crop growing to have anything to sell. Don't worry about him. He'd gripe even if I didn't make any changes. Since I am, it's a betrayal of all the lessons he tried to pass on to me. I just wish he'd take Mom on a trip somewhere, like Alaska. That might be far enough away. They should go on a trip to see the new state, right?"

"Or maybe Hawaii. It's actually the newest state, and it's a lot warmer. I'm sure he'd find something there to keep him interested, like pineapple farms." Nate slapped Martin on the back. "I'm heading out to the creek to check our irrigation system. I don't want the new owner of James Farm to think they have free range on our water."

"I'll stop in and visit as soon as the new owner arrives. I'm surprised they haven't contacted anyone yet about selling the property. I hope we can get a bid in before anyone else talks to him. Expanding our acreage would be a game changer. Can you imagine how much more corn we could grow in those strawberry fields?"

He turned toward the James Farm and thought about all the fun he'd had with Fred James. Martin been a regular over at his house from the time his mom would let him run across the fields. His dad hadn't wanted a kid around the farm, slowing him down, but Fred always treated him like an adult. Now he was gone, and all Martin had was his memories of their adventures.

"I'll miss the old guy though," he continued. "You know Fred taught me how to drive a tractor. And ride a horse. I think I planted most of that lower strawberry field on my own."

"From the way your dad's been going on about his family lessons, I would have thought he taught you those things." Nate grinned as he jumped into his old truck. "Just joshing you. I know you were close to Fred. It's a shame he left without having any kids to take on his legacy."

Martin climbed into his truck to drive back to his house on the other side of the ranch. His father grumbled about the farmland he'd appropriated, but his parents told him he could build where he wanted. His mom had hoped he'd take the field behind them so she could be close to any future grandkids. He told people who asked about the location that he'd chosen it because the building site was flat and near the creek that ran through that part of the farm. Large oak trees framed the creek bank, making the site pretty as well as functional.

When he got back to his house, his mother's car pulled in behind him. She was probably bringing him food. She didn't think he could survive without her feeding him. And he had to admit, he did appreciate the food and the gallons of sweet tea she brought him weekly. It looked like she'd continue the deliveries at least until he got a proper wife. Her words, not his.

He walked back to the Buick and opened her door, reaching out his hand to help her stand. "Hey Mom, what brings you over to this side of the farm?"

"Like you don't know. I brought you a few dinners." Savannah Oaks was a proper Georgia debutante when she married Martin's father, and she'd brought Southern cooking to the Midwest. Or at least to Peculiar. "I wanted to tell you the news I heard in town. Fred's heir is supposed to arrive this afternoon. I guess they're driving here, so they must live in Saint Louis or somewhere close. Cindy at the bank, you know her, right? She's blond, very pretty, single, and adores you. She was two years behind you in school. Anyway, she said Howard said that the new owner should be coming in any day now, according to the phone call Jacob Stine received. I guess bank managers and lawyers keep tabs on this kind of thing." She opened the back door. "Be a dear and grab the tea. I can carry in the other containers."

Martin grabbed a large box as well as the tea jar. The last container held a cake. What he needed with an entire layer cake, he didn't know. His mom must think he invited all the farmhands for coffee and dessert after the workday ended. "You don't have to do this, Mom."

"I know, but I like knowing you have more than just a sandwich to eat." She carried the cake box up on the porch and into the house, aiming straight for the kitchen.

He'd cleaned it last night after he'd eaten dinner, so the only thing in the sink was a bowl for his cereal and a coffee cup. She set the cake on the counter and looked around. "You're not eating all your meals at Sally's, are you?"

"No, Mom. I cooked a steak last night with a baked potato. I even opened a can of green beans to go with it." He put the tea in the fridge then opened a cabinet and took out an empty gallon jar and a Tupperware container. "All clean. I'll put these in your car."

"If I wasn't on the way to the library, I'd think you were trying to get rid of me." She leaned over and kissed his cheek then wiped off the lipstick she'd left before sliding her white gloves on her hands. "I'll see you Sunday?"

"Of course. I'll be at the house at ten after." He walked her to the door then waited while she started the car and backed out of the drive. He loved his mom dearly. He loved his dad too, but sometimes he was hard to deal with.

He made himself a sandwich and poured a glass of sweet tea then took his lunch to the dining room table, which was covered in papers. He had a survey map of his farm as well as the James Farm. He'd been trying to figure out if he needed to buy the water rights as well as the farmland. Maybe the new owner would sell him everything but the farmhouse. He didn't need the two-story house, especially not since he'd built his own too-large, three-bedroom home here on the creek.

He worked on his proposal for the new owner as he ate. All he could be was prepared. By the time that car pulled into town with the new owner, Martin Oaks would be prepared for anything. He was certain.

Chapter Two

As soon as Rhoda got off the bus that night, she dropped her purse and lunch bag in her apartment. Taking a container of water and humming to herself, she climbed the stairs to the roof and continued her discussion with herself about what her life might look like on a farm. The cons came first. She had a stable job here. She had insurance, a pension, and maybe a future. It might not be groundbreaking or interesting work, but she was doing something important. Or at least she thought she was. She didn't know anyone in Missouri. Of course, she didn't really know anyone here either.

And what did she know about farmers? They might see her attempt to run a farm by herself as weird. She opened the door to the roof and then sucked in a breath and stared at what met her eyes.

All the pots she'd carefully planted a few months ago had been thrown against the brick wall. One pot had even been tossed over the wall and onto the neighboring building's roof and was now just a dirt pile with a broken clay pot and a dead plant on top. All the watering and watching as the seeds grew in the pots she'd bought at the closest hardware store, gone. A store she had to take two Saturday buses to get to so she could buy the seeds, planting soil, and clay pots.

All that money, that energy, gone.

Tears fell from her eyes as she gathered the tiny plants. They were in shock and needed soil and water. Her own shock couldn't be solved by just taking a bath and eating dinner, but she might be able to save the plants. She glanced around the empty rooftop and wondered where the kids were that had done this. Were they home, doing homework and eating dinner with their parents? The fun of the destruction they caused now a fleeting memory or a hope that they didn't get caught? She pressed her lips together and wiped her cheeks. She could talk to Clarence and ask him if he'd seen anyone. But that wouldn't bring her plants back. She returned to her apartment and repotted the withered tomatoes. As she worked, she started planning her new life.

Rhoda called in sick the next day, shocking April, since that had never happened before. That morning, she sat at her small kitchen table, watching the day arrive around her and waiting for the office of the attorney in Missouri to open. As she waited, she made a list of questions to ask.

After assuring the surprised Mr. Stine that, no, she didn't want to consider the several offers to sell the property and that she'd be arriving there soon, she started her escape plan. Over the next two weeks, she boxed up all her belongings, including the houseplants she'd brought from her parents' house. She took a vacation day the next week, rode a bus out to the suburbs, and bought a bright red car with a white top. She used her savings for this purchase, hoping the inheritance would at least cover the vehicle's cost.

The last Friday, she drove to her office building and cleaned out her desk at the end of the day. Then she handed April a letter with her forwarding address she'd gotten from the Missouri lawyer. They would need it to send her final paycheck.

The look on April's face was priceless as she questioned Rhoda's decision. "I can't believe you're really serious. Well, I knew you said you were leaving when you gave notice, but I never thought you'd go through with it. What about your future? Who's going to put food on your table and pay your rent?"

Rhoda thought the bigger question in April's head was who was going to do Rhoda's work at the office. The other clerks watched as she packed her few personal belongings. She left the small certificate she'd been given at her fifth anniversary in lieu of a raise in the desk drawer. When she'd first learned of her inheritance, she'd been tempted to simply drop a resignation letter off with security and walk out that same day. But she could never do something like that.

"Thanks for everything, and I hope you have a great career." Rhoda smiled at April, who still stood by what had been Rhoda's desk. She picked up the fern she'd brought in to give her desk a bit of life, walked away, and entered the elevator. From now on, the farm would be her career. She didn't know what she'd be growing or selling, but she'd figure it out. And, as a bonus, she wouldn't have to wear her drab office dresses anymore.

The entire drive to Missouri, Rhoda kept the top up on her new convertible. The wind still blew in the cracks, but it kept the random rainstorms from soaking her and her belongings. Hopefully, the farm would have a more practical truck for her use. The car had been an impulse buy, and now she was regretting it. She'd been running on emotion since Mr. Henry had called her into his office two weeks ago.

Would she soon also regret her decision to quit her job, pack up her apartment, and buy a car to move to the Midwest? This definitely hadn't been on her now defunct five-year plan. Rhoda had never been so impulsive in her life. In spite of all that, though, this change felt right. Or it had.

As she turned down the road that was supposed to take her to the James Farm, her heart beat faster and she regretted everything. She tried to slow her breathing. Worst case, she'd sell the place and move to another city where she could start over. Maybe someplace a little smaller than Baltimore. Anything was better than the life she'd had.

"We're going to be just fine. Right, Candy?" She leaned back to check on the only tomato plant that seemed to have survived the trip. Candy's roots must not have been as damaged as her siblings'. Rhoda wasn't giving up on the other four plants, whose names she didn't remember now. But their survival didn't look promising.

She watched as she drove by a large farmhouse with a wide front porch where two rocking chairs swayed in the breeze. The house looked happy and was surrounded by plants and bushes and a front yard so green, it glistened in the sun. The number on the box said 400 SHADY BROOK LANE. Not her house then. She sped back up and headed to another house she could see in the distance.

When she arrived, she checked the number on the box against the one the lawyer had given her. 680 SHADY BROOK LANE. The name JAMES was also painted on the side, but the lettering was faded and flaking off. She'd clean that up this week and replace JAMES with GREY. She had the first to-do item for her list.

Rhoda turned the convertible up the driveway that was bordered by fields and followed the dirt road up a hill. The white two-story farmhouse came into view quickly once she crested the hill. She parked in front of the house and climbed out of the car. The late spring sun was warm as she reached into the back and grabbed the box with the plants. She'd water them first, before going inside to see her new home.

She glanced around. The large barn sat behind the parking area, and the fields surrounded the house. One field, near the back, had been recently plowed and planted. Tiny green sprouts were popping up all over it. The other had small plants close to the ground. Red berries clung to the vines. Strawberries. She had an entire field filled with strawberries.

"Now isn't this wonderful?" she whispered to Candy, who seemed to be enjoying the bright sunlight. Rhoda set the box at the foot of the porch steps where a row of roses had been planted in a flower bed. The key was supposed to be somewhere on the porch under a mat. She climbed the steps. The house needed some work. Some of the paint had flaked off the railings and the siding, but the bones of the house looked solid. She bounced on her toes to check the porch's construction. Sturdy.

The key was indeed under the welcome mat. She unlocked the door and stepped inside. A warm feeling overwhelmed her, and she realized as she looked around that the few rooms she could see were bigger than her entire apartment. Pictures of couples lined the walls in the hallway, and she recognized her maternal grandparents in one. Uncle Frederick had believed in family. Which must be why she was here. She removed drop cloths from furniture as she walked through the rooms and put them in piles near the doors. She'd deal with them later. First, water for the plants and maybe some for her too. If the well worked.

Rhoda moved from the parlor to the dining room and finally found the kitchen. She walked to the cupboard and got a glass then went to the sink and turned the faucet. The water ran clear and cold, a great sign, so she took a hesitant sip. It smelled and tasted just fine. Uncle Frederick must have kept his well clear. There was so much she needed to learn about living on a farm—including how to cook with gas. She touched the old stove. She'd always used an electric range before.

A sound brought her out of her mental list-building, and she took the glass of water back out front to divide between the plants. A car came up the dirt road—a blue Buick with a very blond woman sitting in the driver's seat. Now Rhoda didn't feel quite as out of place driving her new Ford on these dirt roads. She finished watering and set the glass on the porch railing. Then she walked down the steps and onto the driveway to meet her first visitor.

The woman climbed out of the car. "Good afternoon. I can't believe you're already here. And you drove all the way alone? I'm Savannah Oaks. My husband and I are your closest neighbors. Our unmarried son, Martin, lives near the back of our property."

Great. Rhoda was used to the people at work trying to set her up with every relative over six feet tall. And now it was happening again. Or maybe the woman was just being thorough in her descriptions. Hopefully, this Savannah wasn't looking for a girl-next-door bride for her son. "I'm Rhoda. Rhoda Grey. My uncle left the farm to me."

"Rhoda, such a pretty name. We, of course, knew Fred well. It was such a shame when he died. He attended church with us for years. He and Martin were very close." She turned back to the car, pulled out a gallon jar, and handed it to Rhoda. "Now, I know you don't want to stand out here chatting after driving such a long way in that pretty car of yours. I'm just dropping off some sweet tea, cookies, and some dinner. I wouldn't want to cook after such a long drive. I hear you came all the way from Baltimore. I brought enough to keep you from starving until you get to the grocery store. We have a small one here in Peculiar, but if you want something specific, you'll probably have to go to Kansas City. We're pretty basic out here."

Savannah kept talking about the area and Uncle Frederick, no, Uncle Fred, and where Rhoda could find things, both in town and on the farm. When they reached the kitchen, she put the meal she'd prepared in the fridge and picked up the tea from the table where Rhoda had set it. "Oh my, I should have asked if you even like sweet tea. A lot of people here prefer their tea unsweetened. Although I have no idea how they drink it that way."

Rhoda wasn't quite sure what her new neighbor was talking about. "I've never had sweet tea."

"Well, it's an acquired taste. If you don't like it, let me know, and I'll show you how to make unsweetened sun tea. In my opinion, it's not as good, but to each their own." She glanced at her watch. "I've got to go. My husband, Chet, will be looking for his dinner promptly at six, and I haven't even started anything for our meal yet."

"Oh, I'm sorry to be a bother." Rhoda followed her to the front door.

Savannah spun on her heel quickly. "Oh, Rhoda, you are definitely not a bother. Come to Sunday dinner. We eat at one sharp. Chet does have his routines. I think we need to get some meat on your bones if you're going to take on running this farm."

Rhoda stepped outside and watched as Savannah made a big turn in the driveway then drove away. She looked down at her car, which still needed to be unpacked and decided to try out some sweet tea first. Then she'd get to work.

Sunday morning, Martin was coming back from early services when the red convertible whizzed past him. The woman driving had a scarf over her head and dark sunglasses. News around town was her hair was blond and her eyes were a bright blue and she was very tall, but he hadn't found the time to verify any of those facts. Or to speak with her. He hadn't seen the need when he'd heard the news. According to his mother, Rhoda Grey wasn't planning on selling the farm or leaving Peculiar anytime soon.

Johnny at the hardware store had reported to Nate that Miss Grey had bought some lumber and paint yesterday, but she hadn't told him what she needed the supplies for—and he'd even hinted around the subject. The purchase bothered Martin. The last time he had visited James Farm, Fred had been concerned about a loose board on the back porch. Hopefully, the board hadn't busted and she hadn't gotten hurt. He'd stop by there after he ate dinner with his folks and introduce himself. He touched the envelope that held his offer for Fred's farm. He'd kept it in his truck since the day Miss Grey showed up. Just in case he ran into her. Or worked up the nerve to approach her about selling. All he could do was try. The worst she could do was say no.

He made the turn into the driveway that would lead to his house. He had some reading to finish up before heading to Kansas City to attend the seminar. He wanted to be as knowledgeable as possible about the new herbicide they were pitching. High yield wasn't a positive if the produce was tainted in some way. And his dad still needed to be convinced that they should try the new product.

Information was power only if the person you were trying to inform was willing to listen. Or trust the son he'd turned the farm over to. The way his dad talked, it seemed he thought Martin was likely to tank the entire acreage and poison the land, stripping generations to come of their family income.

His dad could catastrophize with the best of them. Martin chose instead to focus on the possibilities. Which, in his dad's eyes, made him a dreamer.

How did he get so far down this rabbit hole? It didn't matter what his dad thought. Martin was in charge of running the farm now. And he had to make the right decisions.

He poured a glass of sweet tea and settled at the table to work.

When he finished, he glanced at the grandfather clock standing against the dining room wall. His mother had decorated the house before she'd let him move in. The decor was traditional, heavy, and not his taste at all. He would have chosen less stuffy furniture. He assumed his dad had been part of the team, but if he had his way, he'd lighten everything up. Including this dining room.

He stopped and closed his eyes. He should be much more grateful. He whispered, "I'm thankful for my house and all the furniture in it."

Time to go to dinner with the folks and, hopefully, not fight with his father.

When he got to his parents' house, he walked through the dining room and noticed the table was set for four. His mom must have invited Pastor Thomas to dinner. At least he could hope it was Pastor Thomas and that they weren't trying to matchmake again. His mom had surprised him several times by inviting single parishioners in her women's group. He pushed the thought away as he walked through the dining room to the kitchen where his mother was getting everything ready. He handed her the bunch of roses he'd cut from the plant growing near the back of his house. He'd gotten the cuttings from Fred a few years ago, and the bush was finally producing the long-stemmed flowers like its mother plant on the James Farm. "Hey, Mom."

She looked up and smiled. "My dear, you didn't have to bring me flowers. But you know I love them. Get me a vase from that last cabinet, would you?"

"Sure." He got the vase and filled it with water. "Do you want to arrange them?"

She put another cube of butter into the hot potatoes she was mashing. "Go ahead. And while you're doing that, tell me again where you're going next week and when will you be back?"

"I'm going to Kansas City tonight for an herbicide seminar, and I'll be back late on Tuesday." He took some scissors out of the drawer and, after trimming the stems, started setting the roses in the water, one at a time. "Don't worry. I won't stay in the bad part of town, hang out in the saloons, or eat from the hot dog stands. The seed company is hosting, so most of my meals will be at the hotel where the event is being held."

"You be careful. I hate having you go to these things alone. Maybe you should take your dad?" She met his gaze, hopeful.

"No way. You just want him out of your hair." He held out the finished arrangement. "How's this?"

"Perfect. Now go set it on the table. And will you be a lookout for our guest?" His mother smiled at him.

"Please tell me you didn't invite Sunny Holder from church." He set the flowers down. "We've talked about this. If I want to go out with a woman, I'll ask her myself."

"I didn't invite Sunny, although she's a lovely woman and perfect for you. Did you know she's won the peach preserves category at the summer fair three years running?"

"Mom..." He let the word hang there.

"Fine. I won't push. I just want to have grandbabies before I'm dead." She spooned the mashed potatoes into a bowl then put the pan into the sink and ran water into it. "Are you sure you don't want your dad coming with you this week?"

He kissed her on the cheek as he passed by. "Nice try, Mom, but you know Dad and I don't get along when it comes to how to run the farm."

He picked up the flower vase and took it to the dining room. He saw a red convertible sitting out front through the dining room window. If he wasn't mistaken, it was their new neighbor who stood by the car, taking off her scarf. He set the vase on the table, went to the door, and waved to her.

She retrieved a basket from the back seat and came to meet him on the porch. She'd already removed her sunglasses, so when she looked up into his eyes, he could see that the rumors were true. Her eyes were stunningly blue. He stared at her. She wasn't just pretty. She was extraordinary.

She held out the basket. "Hello, I've brought strawberries. I picked them this morning."

"That was kind of you, Miss Grey," he croaked. For some reason, his mouth was bone dry. "Please, come in."

The shock in her eyes surprised him. "Please, call me Rhoda. You already know who I am?"

"Yes, I know who you are. Everyone in town does. You're the first new person in Peculiar for a very long time. I'm Martin Oaks. I've seen you driving down the road in that convertible of yours going to and from your farm." He led her into the dining room. "How do you like the farmhouse? Fred did a lot of remodeling a few years ago. Like adding the laundry room and the second bathroom on the main floor."

"It's very comfortable. And large. I used to live in a one-bedroom apartment in Baltimore. I could practically reach from the kitchen window to the living room couch. And I thought I was being wasteful by not renting a studio apartment. Now, I'm always leaving something downstairs when I need it upstairs and vice versa. My uncle was very generous to leave it to me." Rhoda smiled as she talked about Fred James.

"Hey, Martin." Martin's father came into the dining room. "Rhoda has kindly offered to join us for lunch."

"The pleasure is all mine. I appreciate Savannah's offer of a home-cooked meal." Rhoda beamed at the older Oaks man. "I could have eaten in town though."

"Nonsense. Why eat at Sally's Diner when you can eat my Vanna's food? My wife should be a chef, she's that good. These are lovely. I'm sure Vanna will find something to do with them." He took the basket of strawberries from her and moved toward the kitchen door. "Martin, please show our guest to the living room and entertain her until dinner is served. I'm going to see if I can make myself useful in the kitchen."

Martin stood frozen for a few moments before Rhoda pointed to her left. "I take it that the living room is that way?"

"Yes. Sorry about my manners. I'm not used to being called on to host. My father is usually the one who can't be torn away from visiting with our guests." They moved to the living room and sat on the wing chairs that framed the large stone fireplace. "So, how are you finding your time in Peculiar? I'm sure you're probably ready to get back to the city and all its activities. How long will it take you to make the leasing arrangements?"

She frowned. "I'm not going to lease out anything. I did have offers to sell the property, but I turned them down. I'm planning on working the farm and making Peculiar my home."

"Oh, I didn't realize." He had heard she wasn't planning on selling, but for some reason he hadn't expected this answer. Most of the women he knew wanted out of farm life with all of its dirt and work. This one, she planned on staying. He wondered if she knew anything about farming. He decided to be up front with her. "I have to admit, I've been looking at expanding Oaks Farm. I've taken over the management of the family lands this last year. If you're ever thinking of selling, I'd love to talk with you."

"I'm not sure you heard me." Rhoda sat up straighter. "I'm not selling the farm. I'm here to stay."

He watched her for a minute, admiring the strength of her resolve. "Running a farm is hard work."

"I'm not afraid of hard work." She glanced at her hands. "My mother taught me how to garden as soon as I was old enough to tell a weed from a flower. I'm staying put."

"Well, I should hope so." Mom came into the living room and set a pitcher of tea and four glasses of ice on the coffee table. "You just got here. You haven't experienced all the joys of life in a small town. My women's group has a book club you're more than welcome to join. We're reading a mystery this month, *Cat Among the Pigeons*, by Agatha Christie. It's very suspenseful."

Martin wondered if his mother realized their new neighbor was just as much of a mystery as the fictional one in her book.

Chapter Three

Someone had torn down her sign. Just yesterday, Rhoda and Steve Andrus, her uncle's farmhand, had put up a COMING SOON sign with JAMES FARM U-PICK carefully painted in red and black and several hand-drawn strawberries on it. The sign had looked cute. Now it lay on the ground in the dirt.

She picked up the sign and dusted it off. It wasn't broken, just a little dirty. She glanced at the skies. Maybe there had been a freak windstorm. Or maybe she hadn't put enough nails in it to keep the sign securely on the pole. A memory of the destroyed tomato pots on the rooftop hit her, making her heart race. She leaned the sign against Uncle Fred's old pickup she'd brought out this morning with the rest of the wood to build a small shed and a table.

Rhoda sat on the tailgate and took a deep breath. Maybe she was overreacting. The sign could have fallen. A noise brought her head up, and she saw a tractor in the next field. The one that bordered her property with Oaks Farm. Martin had seemed shocked when she'd told him on Sunday that she wasn't leasing or selling. Just like Jacob Stine had been when he'd visited last week to finalize the estate.

Martin Oaks. Well, if his mother was in a matchmaking mood, he'd be married off soon. The man looked like someone who lived in one of those romance books people left in the break room at work.

She'd picked one up and was hooked right away by the story that transported her to medieval times and stone castles. She felt an attraction to this man who wanted to buy her property. Especially when he gazed into her eyes and smiled. She blinked away the memory.

Maybe they were right. Maybe running James Farm alone was a pipe dream. She closed her eyes and listened to the sounds around her. Then she was reminded of something her mother had always told her. She opened her eyes and said to the farm, "I am strong. I can do anything I set my mind to do." Rhoda left off the last part of the saying her mother had added, "I am loved." Right now, she didn't have anyone to love her. Her parents were gone. The uncle she'd never known was gone. She didn't have family. But she was developing friends and a new life here. And a random windstorm or a grumpy neighbor wasn't going to change her mind.

A truck was coming down the road, and she recognized the man driving. Steve. She'd rehired him to work around the farm after he stopped by to see if she needed some help. He told her that he'd worked for her uncle and would appreciate her employing him. After checking his references and talking to Savannah, she'd called him last week.

He parked on the side of the road and came over to her truck. "What happened to the sign?"

"Good question. I'm not sure." She slipped off the tailgate. "I guess we'll just have to rehang it. Ready to build a shed and a table?"

He grinned and picked up the sign. "I'll get this hung back up, and then we'll get busy. We need to get some income flowing into your farm or you won't be able to pay me."

By the end of the day, both the sign and the shed were up. Steve left her at the house and went to set water for the evening on the top field. They had established a rotation to make sure at least one of the strawberry fields was dry enough each day to have people traipsing through. She needed to paint the shed so the wood wouldn't rot. And tomorrow, she'd go around town and post signs for their grand opening on Saturday. The list went on and on. She went to the kitchen to heat up soup for dinner and to go over her business plan one more time.

Steve was right, she needed some income. So far, all she'd done was spend money. But if she could get enough customers this weekend, she might be able to think about planting blueberries in the fall. And the section near the creek was perfect for some apple trees. If she did it right, in five to ten years the farm would be fully functioning and she should be able to put money away. Thank goodness her uncle had believed in a rainy-day fund. She was pleasantly surprised when she went to the bank the first day to set up everything in her name. Now all she needed was a good season.

Steve knocked at the screen door.

She walked over and opened it, motioning him inside. "I thought you were heading home."

"I was, but I wasn't able to set the water. Someone dumped dirt into your ditch. It's too dark tonight to get it cleared out, but I'll come early tomorrow. We won't have a lot of time before we'll have to turn it off, but we can probably get half the field watered." He held his hat in his hands. "I'm beginning to think we've got an issue here."

She leaned against the doorway. "I'm beginning to think you're right. Thanks for letting me know."

Steve examined the door latches. "Make sure you lock up at night, okay? Just to be safe."

She shivered but nodded. "I'll see you tomorrow. Stop by, and I'll make you breakfast for coming out so early."

He grinned. "I'd appreciate that. Tina's not much for getting up early now that she's got the baby finally sleeping through the night. I was dreading telling her I was going to be working early."

"Tell Tina to stay in bed. I'll feed you tomorrow." She watched as Steve strolled back to his truck, and then she shut and locked the door. The chicken noodle soup was boiling, so she shut off the gas then went to the front and locked that door as well. She didn't want to be paranoid, but like Steve had said, better to be safe.

She stared out at the glowing lights of the Oaks farmhouse. Was her problem closer than she knew? If Martin thought a few childish pranks would scare her off, he had another think coming. Tomorrow morning, after getting Steve settled, she'd go visit Martin Oaks and tell him to grow up or expect a call from the sheriff. She knew how to deal with bullies. Show no fear.

Except Martin hadn't seemed like a bully. He'd been nice to her at his parents' house and was genuinely interested in her plans for the farm. Or at least she'd thought he was. He seemed resigned to the fact that she wasn't going to sell. His brown eyes looked kind when they'd locked gazes passing the mashed potatoes at dinner.

She shook her head. No use mooning over some man who might be trying to sabotage her farm. Still, the sight of his smiling face

in Peculiar, Missouri

Sunday stayed with her as she went back to the kitchen to eat her supper and study her business plan.

Martin had gotten home from Kansas City late Tuesday night after sitting through the seminar, which was mostly a badly veiled push to buy their seed. Now he sat in his kitchen eating breakfast and rethinking his planting schedule for the next year—one that didn't involve annexing the James Farm acreage. Rhoda Grey had been adamant that she wasn't going to sell. At least until she figured out that the farm was too much and decided to head back east to civilization. So he was stuck with what he had. He hadn't befriended Fred James because he assumed he'd get the land, but he *had* envisioned a day when he'd add that acreage to his farm plan.

And that was what happened when a farmer counted his chickens before they hatched. He refocused on the paper in front of him. Then he drew a huge *X* on it and took out a clean sheet. He'd have to start all over.

A car pulled up in front of the house, and Bo started barking and took off. He'd been out back, relaxing just outside the kitchen screen door while Martin worked. Martin turned off the radio he'd been playing in the kitchen and followed Bo around the house.

The red convertible was parked in his driveway. Bo had his feet on the driver's door and was getting a head rub from Rhoda. Martin smiled as he approached the car. "He's usually a better watchdog than this, but he seems to like you."

She faced him, and her smiled dropped. "I'm good with animals."

He leaned on the porch rail. "What can I do for you today?"

She turned back to Bo and said, "Okay, let me out, buddy. I need to talk to your master."

To Martin's surprise, Bo complied with her command and, wagging his tail, came to sit by Martin's side. He reached down and scratched the dog's ears. "Good boy."

Rhoda opened the car door, and Martin focused on her tennis shoes showing tan ankles. For some reason, the sight intrigued him. He looked down at Bo, letting her get out of the vehicle without being gawked at.

Once the car door slammed, he looked up and watched her stomp over to him. This wasn't going to be pretty. The woman was hopping mad. He imagined he could see steam coming out the top of her head, which was only a couple inches shorter than his.

"Mr. Oaks. I can't believe you would stoop so low as to destroy my property. That's not going to get you any closer to owning my farm. I've told you no, I'm not selling, and I mean it." She put her hands on her hips, and he noticed she was dressed in a white button-down without sleeves and green capris. Even in the heat of the morning, she looked cool.

And why was he thinking about the way she looked? He processed her words. "What? What happened at the farm? What was destroyed?"

She stared at him, trying to see something in his face. All he felt was confusion.

Finally, she sank against the car. "Where were you last night and the night before?"

in Peculiar, Missouri

"Kansas City." He walked over and leaned next to her. "Remember? I mentioned my trip at the dinner table on Sunday. And then my dad made fun of my newfangled farming methods? I got back late last night. I didn't want to be away from the farm too long. What's going on?"

He could see the mental gymnastics going on in her head. She surely remembered the conversation, because it had become uncomfortable and tense until his mother had changed the subject to talk about her book club again.

"You weren't here?" She sank even deeper onto the car.

"I wasn't in town. But you're clearly upset about something. Come sit on the porch, and we'll talk about this over a cup of coffee. I just made a pot." He motioned to the two rocking chairs. "I'm a good listener, I promise."

She pushed back a lock of hair that had fallen out of her long braid. "I'd like some coffee."

He hurried inside, poured two cups of coffee, and then opened the fridge. He didn't have any milk or cream. He grabbed the sugar bowl and put it, the two cups, and a spoon on a tray. He went back to the front door. The living room was a mess and still had his opened suitcase on the couch where he'd left it last night. Thank goodness he hadn't asked her inside. He pushed the screen door open and saw Bo with his head on Rhoda's lap. "He really likes you."

"He's a good dog. I haven't had a dog since high school." She met his gaze. "My apartment building didn't allow pets."

"I've had Bo for years. I hate to think about how old he's getting. I don't want to jinx it." Martin set the tray down and handed her a cup. "I'm hoping you take it black or with sugar, since that's all I've got. I need to hit the grocery store soon."

"Black's fine." She sipped the coffee. "I had some trouble over at the farm."

"I gathered that. What happened?"

"Monday morning I found the road sign I'd put up for the U-pick season on the ground. I thought maybe it was the wind. Steve and I built the new stand on Monday, and I painted it yesterday. Anyway, Monday night, we had more issues. Someone dumped dirt in my irrigation ditch. Steve had to dig it out Tuesday morning to get half the watering time we needed." She stared at him as she told the story. "And all this is news to you. I can see it on your face."

"You thought since I told you I wanted to buy the farm that I'd try to drive you out?" He looked at Bo, who lay by Rhoda's feet. "That's not who I am or how I'd get what I want. I asked if you were selling the farm, and you said no. So I asked you to keep me in mind if you decide to sell later. That's all."

"Someone wants my farm to fold. And you did want the land." She shrugged. "You had to be first on my list."

Martin recalled Nate's comments about the James Farm and their water. He shook his head. "Not me. But I'll talk to my farm manager and see if he's had similar problems. It might be kids playing pranks. The farm was left sitting for a few weeks while Jacob tried to find you."

She sighed. "Kids. It's always kids. Don't people even care what their kids are doing anymore? I expected this in Baltimore. Kids ran the streets. I guess some of them were in gangs, but most were just bored."

"*West Side Story* in Baltimore?" He smiled at her shocked look. "Yes, we get newspapers out here and hear about cultural events like plays and music, even if we have to go out of town to watch anything. Except the high school puts on a play every year. Last year they did *South Pacific*. It was good."

He could tell she wasn't really listening, just thinking through what he'd said. "Look, let me talk to Nate. If he hasn't noticed anything, I'll go with you to talk to the sheriff. I'm not sure he'll be able to do anything, but he might have an idea of which kids might be responsible."

"You'd do that? Help me find out who's doing this?"

He nodded and picked up his coffee. There was more than one reason he'd volunteer to help out his neighbor. He was simply being a good Christian and following the example of Christ, for one. But he had an ulterior motive as well. He would get to stay close to Rhoda. He had a feeling he needed to be there. He just hoped it was his head telling him to help out and not his heart. "Tell me about your plans. Are you staying focused on strawberries?"

He could see her calm down as she talked about James Farm and her plans for the future. She had a good head on her shoulders. But he wasn't sure about a roadside stand or this U-pick market-delivery method. What if people tore up her plants? He kept his concerns to himself as she talked.

She picked up her cup and saw it was empty. She stood, and Bo jumped up as well. "I'm sorry, I've kept you from your work."

He stood also and set his cup on the tray. "No, really, I was just revising next year's forecast. Without your extra acres."

She laughed and moved toward the steps. "That's a good sign, at least for me."

"Look, there's a carnival setting up out on Quarry Road for the weekend. It's the spring festival, so most of the town will be there at some time or other during the weekend. They have flower contests, food, and rides. Would you like to attend? I can pick you up, maybe Friday night?"

She paused at her car. "I'll have to be back early. I'm doing my first U-pick day on Saturday."

"I'm sure we'll be able to see everything and still have you home at a respectable hour." He leaned on the porch rail, watching her. "It's a small event."

She opened her car door and met his gaze. "I'd love to."

Then it's a date. He waved as she drove away. Now he just needed to make sure Nate wasn't pulling any tricks on the new neighbor. If his hired hand was responsible for the pranks, he'd have to set him straight.

Chapter Four

Rhoda lifted her coffee cup and stared at the piles of books, papers, and notes from her uncle stacked on the dining room table. Her mother would be appalled that Rhoda didn't pack everything up after the day's work, but there was just too much. Uncle Fred had first thought of the idea of a U-pick harvest plan years ago but hadn't put it in place. The concept was easy. Charge people to go in the field and pick as many strawberries as they wanted and charge them by the pound. The implementation, that was a little trickier. She either needed to be open only on the weekends and maybe Wednesday, or she needed to figure out a way for someone, which meant her, to be in two places at once.

And then there was the little issue of Oaks Farm and their possible interference with her farm. Martin hadn't actually done the vandalism, but something in his eyes—his deep brown eyes—made her wonder if he knew who the culprit was.

She stood and went to the kitchen to refill her coffee then looked out the window over the sink. A Cadillac was driving toward the house. The dust from the mostly dirt roads out in the country was caked on the car's windows. She set her cup down and went out to greet the new arrival. Either the driver was lost, or it was another town resident come to welcome her to Peculiar. She had two casseroles in the fridge and a pile of cookies in her kitchen from recent "visits." Rhoda figured she was the new sideshow, since townsfolk all wanted to meet the woman who thought she could run a farm.

A man in a suit got out and cast a squinted look around the farm. His gaze landed on her, and his mouth turned up into a large smile. Like the Cheshire cat from the Disney movie, *Alice in Wonderland*. A cold chill ran down Rhoda's spine, but she pushed the feeling away and stepped off the porch to greet him. "Good morning. How can I help you?"

"I'm looking for the new owner of James Farm. I assume you're Rhododendron Grey?" He stepped forward, his hand outstretched.

"That's me. But please, call me Rhoda. My mother loved flowers." She shook the man's hand. It felt soft, and he had a weak grip. "And you are…"

"Oh, sorry, forgive my manners." He made a quick bow as he dropped her hand. "I'm the mayor of Peculiar, Terrance Powers. My friends call me Terry."

"Nice to meet you." She nodded to the porch. "Do you have time for coffee or an iced tea?"

"Of course. I'd love some coffee. No cream, no sugar." He followed Rhoda to the porch and held the screen door open for her. When he followed her inside, she turned, a little confused. "I'm just helping with the drinks. No worries. Fred and I went way back. I know what a mess he left this house in for you. But you've done a great job digging out from the chaos. Fred loved to hold on to a lot of things. I'm surprised you could make your way inside the house."

Rhoda didn't contradict her guest, but the house had been in good shape when she'd pulled in the driveway that first time. She led him to the dining room on her way to the kitchen.

"I guess you're still in cleaning mode." He waved a hand at the table.

"I'm using it as my desk as well as a table." She moved a pile of papers from one end and pointed to a chair. Please make yourself comfortable. Coffee, black, right?"

"Exactly." He beamed at her. "You have an excellent memory."

She didn't point out that he'd told her the information just a moment ago. "I'll be right back."

She refilled her cup that she'd brought into the kitchen and then filled a second one. Then she returned to the dining room. The mayor hadn't sat down. Instead, he was looking through her notes on the farm. He obviously hadn't heard her come back into the room. "Here we go," she said.

He flushed and dropped the papers onto the table. "Sorry. I'm always interested in what other people are doing. I guess it's an occupational hazard. If I don't know my townspeople, how can I best serve them?"

"I guess you'll just have to actually talk to them." She set the coffee down and sat at the opposite end of the table where she'd asked him to sit.

He hurried over to settle next to her and sipped his coffee. "Very good. I love strong coffee. Some of my constituents seem to like it weak. I hate that."

"Me too." She watched him. "So, what can I help you with?"

"I came out to meet you." He smiled and set the cup on the table. "Okay, you caught me. My wife and I have been looking for a retirement farm. I'm sure I won't be Peculiar's mayor for much longer. She wants me home more. And I hate campaigning every four years."

"I'm not selling." She decided it was better to just be up front. What was it with everyone here in Peculiar? Why did everyone think she wanted the money?

"Oh, I guess I assumed. I'd give you a fair price. You could either hold an auction for the farm equipment, or I would get it appraised and give you that money too." He leaned forward. "Farming is a hard way to make a life."

"But not a retirement?" Rhoda challenged his statement. He had assumed that because she was a woman, she wouldn't be interested in growing things. Yet she'd never felt more at home.

He laughed and picked up his cup. "My wife thinks working a farm will keep me healthy. I won't be behind my desk or driving somewhere all the time. So it's perfect for a retirement life. We don't need to have a good crop each year. We have some cushion."

"I'm glad for you. But the farm isn't for sale. I'm sorry you wasted your time driving out here." She raised her eyebrows. "Was there anything else?"

"No, just to welcome you to Peculiar. Are you going to the festival this weekend?" His face had that same Cheshire cat smile. It hadn't faltered at all during the entire conversation. Her mother had once told her to never trust a person who smiled too much. Rhoda hadn't known what that meant until this moment.

"I'm going on Friday." She made it sound casual, not date-like. "I'm looking forward to meeting more people."

He glanced around the room one last time before he stood. "Splendid. I'm sure I'll see you there."

After she'd walked him to the porch, she watched him drive away. He hadn't been happy when she'd turned down his offer to

in Peculiar, Missouri

buy the place. Friday she was going to ask Martin what was going on with the farm. Was there gold buried in the fields?

She waved at Steve, who was coming out of the barn with a bucket. He'd told her she needed to seed her grass in the yard before the current grass gave up. It was supposed to rain tonight, so he wanted it done before the rain fell. She went back inside. She'd asked him to set her up a patch near the barn where she could start some herbs, tomatoes, and other veggies. Maybe she'd sell those at the roadside stand in a couple of months. She was almost too late to start a garden, but she'd give it her best. As long as no one messed with the plants.

Right now, she couldn't assume they were safe from that. She'd come here to get away from the random violence in the city streets. Now it seemed she had the same problem. And a bunch of people who wanted to buy the farm. She couldn't help but think the two were connected.

Martin found Nate in the barn, working on the tractor. He'd rehearsed his questions several times last night and hoped he wouldn't sound accusatory. "Hey, what's going on here?"

"The tractor needed a tune-up. I replaced all the spark plugs this morning. When you pay the kind of money you did for these things, you need to take care of them. My father had an old tractor that ran forever, mostly because he babied the beast." Nate crawled out from under the tractor, took a cloth from his pocket, and wiped his hands. "How was Kansas City? Tell me you at least went out to dinner and saw some people. You're never going to find a wife sitting in your hotel room or hanging out at home."

"I'm not looking for a wife. Besides, I don't want to get in the way of my mother's matchmaking. I'm sure she has some Southern belle waiting in the wings for me." He leaned on one of the barn columns. This was silly. Nate was family. He wouldn't damage someone else's property. He took care of the farm better than Martin even knew. But he'd said he'd ask. "Hey, did anything happen while I was gone?"

Nate focused on putting his tools back into the toolbox they kept in the barn, carefully wiping off any traces of grease before putting them where they belonged. "No, it was pretty quiet. Monday night's not our irrigation day, so I left early after everything was done."

"Big plans with that redhead?" Martin hoped he would say yes. If Nate was with his new girlfriend, that would be an alibi. He watched as Nate blushed then walked over to return the toolbox to the shelf.

"Nah, I headed home and heated up some chili for dinner." He shot a glance at Martin. "Why are you so interested?"

Martin shrugged. "Like you've told me many times, I have no life. I live through your adventures. So, you just went home on Monday night? What about Sunday night? Where were you then?"

Nate strode to the door. "You're not my mother. I've got things to do."

Martin stayed in the barn for a bit, pacing. Nate hadn't wanted to tell him where he was, and it was obvious he wasn't home. Maybe Rhoda was right, and someone, like Nate, was trying to ruin her business. He decided he needed more information. He called Bo, and they got into his truck. Then he drove to James Farm.

He climbed out of the truck and waved to Steve. Rhoda was back by the barn, planting. He headed that way, and by the time he and Bo reached her, she stood in the shade, watching him. "Sorry to bother you."

"It's not Friday, right?" She looked down at her dirty knees and then tucked her hands behind her. "Tell me I didn't mess up the days of the week. It's hard out here without going to the office to remind me."

"No." He laughed. "It's not Friday. It's Wednesday. But I wondered if you would mind taking a drive with me this evening."

She blinked. "A drive?"

He stepped closer and looked over his shoulder. Steve and Nate had gone to school together. They might be friends. Everyone knew everyone in Peculiar. "My foreman says he was at home, alone, Monday night."

Rhoda took in the information. "But you don't believe him."

"I want to, but there was something he wasn't telling me. I could see it on his face." He shifted his weight from foot to foot, thinking about what it was Nate could be hiding. "I want to follow him tonight when he leaves my farm."

"And you want me to come along?"

"If he comes over here, you'll have proof of what he's doing, and I'll be a witness for the police. If he goes home, we know he's probably telling the truth." He took his baseball cap off and ran his hand through his hair. "I don't want it to be him. Do you want to come?"

"Sure. I'll play Dick Tracy with you." She leaned down and rubbed Bo's head.

He smiled at the reference. "A little more Sherlock Holmes and Watson. But I'll buy you dinner for your trouble if he just goes home. And if he doesn't, well…"

She picked up a seed packet. "Sounds like a plan, Mr. Oaks. I'll be waiting for your arrival. About five?"

"I'll pick you up at four thirty. Nate usually takes off at five." He put his hat back on and turned toward the truck. "Come on, Bo."

She called after him. "I hope it's not your friend."

"Me too," he said as he got into the cab. "Me too."

Hours later, Martin dropped Bo off at the house just before going to pick up Rhoda. He fed his dog dinner, and when he left, Bo was on the front porch, sleeping. Of course, he would wake up if anyone came by. He was a great guard dog, but he knew when to get his rest. Especially after dinner.

Martin drove to Rhoda's house and found her on the porch. She wore her hair in a ponytail, rather than the braid it had been in that morning. "Thanks for doing this," he said as he opened the passenger-side door for her.

"I appreciate your help. I want to stay here, and in order for that to happen, I need to know who's messing with my farm." She climbed into the truck and settled her purse next to her. She paused a minute, then continued talking when he got into the driver's seat. "I don't want it to be your friend. You clearly care for the guy, but I have to know."

"Believe me, I understand." He turned around and went back down the road, parking the truck on a lane that serviced one of Oaks Farm's cornfields. "He's up on the north field today, so when he leaves, he'll come out the barn road and turn left or right. Left

in Peculiar, Missouri

will take him to town and his place. Right, well, you know where right goes."

He shut off the engine after turning the truck around to watch for Nate. Then he turned the key and switched on the radio. The local station was playing an Elvis song. One of his ballads. He dropped his hand from the radio. "Is this okay? I know some people have issues with rock and roll."

"You're kidding, right? I love all kinds of music. I find some of the newer artists are calming my nerves about the state of the world." She nodded to the radio. "Elvis is from Memphis and loves to sing gospel music. Everyone has something that makes them special."

He leaned on the door, watching her. "So what about you, Rhoda? What makes you special?"

She blushed. "I didn't mean me. I guess I'm like my name, Grey. I fade into the background. I love plants though. It's like they can talk, if you just listen."

"And what do you think they're saying?" he asked, amused.

"I think they might object to your use of herbicides and pesticides on them. You know, there are better ways."

Not according to the seed company. He shrugged. "Fewer weeds and bugs means a better yield on the crops. It's just basic math."

"But if you're damaging the land, where are you going to grow corn next year, or in ten years?" She glanced over at the cornfield to her left and sat up straight.

Martin followed her gaze. The corn wasn't quite tall enough to totally hide them, but it was on a curve, so unless Nate was looking for his truck, he shouldn't see them. What Martin saw was Nate's truck sitting at the edge of the road, waiting for a car to drive past.

He held his breath then groaned. Nate had turned right. He was headed to James Farm. "We'll have to postpone this argument for another day. Nate's coming."

She nodded. "I see him."

Martin waited for Nate's truck to pass them before starting the engine. Then he turned onto the road and followed him, giving him a chance to take one of the several lanes that accessed James Farm. But Nate kept driving. Martin exchanged a look with Rhoda. "You don't know of any other roads that lead to your farmland, right?"

"Not that I know of. Where else could he be going? I didn't think this road went anywhere."

"Years ago it used to be a dead end, but now it attaches to a highway farther out. I didn't think there were other farms out here. Do you mind if we keep following him?"

"In for a penny, in for a pound." She watched as her fields passed by the window. Then they were past her farm, and Nate still hadn't stopped. "Where do you think he's going?"

As soon as she asked, brake lights flashed in front of them. Nate turned his truck into a driveway that led to a small barn and what looked like an even smaller house. Martin slowed down. "Can you see what's on the mailbox?"

She leaned over, looking out her passenger window. "It says T. Jones. Why?"

Martin pointed to a tractor in the driveway, hooked to a plow. "Because that looks a lot like my tractor."

"What are you going to do?" She watched as Nate parked and walked over to greet another man.

Martin watched the two men talk then seemed to make a decision. "You'll probably want to stay in the truck for this conversation. I'm sure it'll get heated."

"I'm not staying in the truck," she said. Martin jerked the steering wheel to the left, and the truck went careening down the dirt driveway. She took a deep breath when it rolled to a stop behind Nate's truck.

Martin jumped out and stormed over to where the men were talking.

Rhoda followed him, ignoring Martin's directions. If these were the men tearing up her farm, she wanted to look them in the eye and confront them.

"Martin, what are you doing here?" Nate asked, standing in front of the other man.

"I could ask you the same question. What are you doing here, and why is my tractor here?" He paused, waiting for an answer.

"Boss, it's not what you think." Nate held out his hands, trying to calm down the situation. "Let me explain."

Martin put his hands on his hips. "Will an explanation include the reason why this isn't grand theft?"

Chapter Five

Rhoda couldn't blame Nate. She might have done the same thing in the situation. Except she would have let the owner of the equipment know about the loan. And she would have asked permission.

"Nate, I would have let you borrow the tractor. You didn't have to hide it from me." Martin glanced around Nate's small family farm.

"I felt like an idiot. I've been so busy making sure Oaks Farm is in shape, I didn't keep our own tractor updated and serviced. So the engine blew, and we can't afford a new one until payments for the harvest come in," Nate explained again.

"Hopefully, we can afford one then," Thomas, Nate's brother, added.

"Look, we'll figure something out." Nate slapped Thomas on the back. "You worry too much."

"And you don't worry enough," Thomas retorted.

So this is what it's like to have a brother, Rhoda thought. They clearly cared for each other, but emotions also ran high between the two men with each of them thinking they were right in the situation. "I have to ask, is this where you were Monday night? Neither of you were at my farm?"

"I've got to get the seed planted or we won't have any crop." Nate looked up at the slowly setting sun. "And, if it's okay, I need to go now and plow."

"Hold on a second. You were both here Sunday and Monday night?" Martin asked again.

"I just told you we were. Why, what's going on?" Nate looked between Martin and Rhoda.

Rhoda explained the issues she'd been having at the farm.

Nate whistled. "So you think someone's trying to get you to leave the farm?"

"Leave and sell. Someone wants that land," Martin said.

Nate shook his head. "The last thing I need is more land to take care of. You were hoping to buy the property off old man James. How do I know you're not accusing me to cover yourself?"

"I was out of town." Martin smiled and reached out a hand to Nate. "Sorry for doubting you."

Nate shook Martin's hand. "And I'm sorry for borrowing your tractor without your permission."

"Just get your crops in, and if you need it again, let me know, okay?" Martin turned to leave, but Thomas stepped forward.

"Hey, you said your irrigation ditch was blocked. Saturday, when I went up to set my pipes, I saw Jacob Stine's car up there. I thought it was weird but assumed he was checking out the place for the new owner." Thomas nodded to Rhoda.

She looked at Martin. Jacob had been helpful as she navigated the things she needed to do regarding the estate. She felt that he didn't totally approve of her trying to run the farm alone, but he hadn't said anything outright. Except that he had a client who would buy the place, as is. "Jacob Stine, the attorney? He was out by the creek?"

Thomas moved toward the tractor with his brother. "That's what I saw."

As Martin drove her back to her house, Rhoda stared out the window. Now she knew three people who hadn't tried to wreck her farm but suspected someone else. She wanted to love this little town. Truly, she did. But someone didn't want her here.

"Penny for your thoughts," Martin said.

She snorted. "That's about all they're worth these days. I was just wondering why it is that every time I start feeling comfortable, someone messes with me. At school, I had a growth spurt in seventh grade, so I was the tallest girl in the class. Add in my crippling shyness, and I was the perfect target for bullies."

"You're not too tall. Did you know that you have to be over five foot six to be a model? My cousin made me measure her every summer once a week when we were kids. She never made it past five foot five and a half. One week she didn't ask me to measure her. She'd decided to round up and they would just have to live with it." He chuckled at the memory.

"Did she become a model?" Rhoda asked.

Martin turned the truck into her driveway and parked in front of her house. "No, she decided to go to college and become a teacher instead. She wanted to teach college, but she fell in love with the boy next door. Now they have five kids, and she teaches English at the high school. My mom shows me the pictures of her kids every time I stop by."

"New pictures? She sends that many?" Rhoda climbed out of the truck, not waiting for him to walk around and open the door.

"No, they're the same pictures. It's just Mom's not-so-subtle hint that I'm getting older and she wants grandchildren." He followed her to the door.

in Peculiar, Missouri

She unlocked the door and swung it open. "Your mother is relentless. She dropped by with a copy of the book her book club is reading so I'd be prepared if I wanted to join her at the next meeting."

"You might have fun." He gestured toward the foyer. "Do you want me to walk through the house before I leave?"

"No. It's a mess, and I'm sure everything is fine. I don't see any signs of a break-in. I think I'm safe."

Concern flickered in his eyes. "Okay then. I'll see you tomorrow morning?"

"Why?" She stepped into the house and dropped her keys into a small wooden box she kept by the door. Then she turned around, leaned on the doorjamb, and watched him.

"I think we should pay your attorney a visit and see why he was at the creek. There's only one reason to be out at that spot, and I don't think he was there to water your crops." Martin leaned down to touch her potted tomato plant. "I thought you were doing a garden?"

"I am, but I brought Candy with me from Baltimore." She picked up a jar of water she kept by the door and stepped out to water the plant.

"Candy? You name your plants?" He watched her pour the water into the pot, clearly amused by the idea.

She stood and replaced the lid on the jar. Then she returned to the front door. "Candy's special. She's the reason I'm here. I'll tell you the story someday. Good evening, Mr. Oaks."

Martin turned into the driveway and saw Rhoda standing on the porch, next to her tomato plant, Candy. Naming plants? Maybe she was a little too granola for him. Next thing he knew, she'd be hosting a group of beatniks for a poetry reading.

She waved when she saw him, and he was ashamed of his negative thoughts. Rhoda was a nice person. He didn't need to be labeling her just because she was a little different than most of the people he knew. Hopefully she didn't name all of her plants, or the introduction phase of their relationship was going to take forever. He parked and met her at the passenger side of the truck as she hurried off the porch. "Good morning. Ready to do some investigating?"

"I'm in my best Nancy Drew outfit, minus the hat. I don't like wearing hats inside. It seems so frivolous." She climbed into the cab.

"I called Jacob Stine's office before I came over, and he'll see us at ten." He started the engine.

"So, we're just walking into his office and asking what he was doing at the creek?" She set a box on the bench seat between them. "What if he lies?"

"Maybe he'll be truthful. I prefer to think that most people are good rather than the opposite." He tapped the box. "What's in here?"

"Cookies for Mr. Stine. An excuse for us to be chatting? I thought it would be nice to thank him for all the work he did on the estate." She opened the box and took out two pinwheel cookies. She handed him one. "Chocolate and vanilla. Who could lie to us after eating a few of these?"

He took a bite of the cookie. Delicious. "I think you have an edge on Nancy Drew. She couldn't bake like this."

"You don't know that. Her baking skills could have been her top-secret weapon that the author didn't want us to know about."

She finished her cookie. "I couldn't sleep last night. I kept watching out the window to see if anyone was sneaking around."

"We'll find out who's been messing with your farm soon enough. Did you see anything last night?" He eyed the box. Maybe he could sneak another cookie without her noticing.

"No. It was all quiet around my house. Your folks had lights on until late though. Everything okay there?" She handed him another cookie out of the box.

"Dad reads after Mom goes to bed. He says it's the only time the house is quiet enough for him to think." He laughed as they passed his parents' house. "When I was in high school, he'd yell at me for staying up late and doing my homework. But I liked reading and working at night. The house was quiet."

"Like father, like son, I guess." She gazed out the window. "I did all my homework as soon as I got home. Then my mom and I would work in the garden. I think she knew that if she let me garden first, I'd never do any of my homework. I was always more comfortable with a little dirt on my hands."

He watched as she clasped her hands together. Changing the subject, he focused on his driving. "Maybe I should loan Bo to you for a while. He's a great guard dog. I think he's bored at my house. He doesn't even have squirrels to chase."

"I'd hate to take your dog."

Even though her words seemed dismissive of the idea, he could see the hope in her eyes as she thought about having a dog around. "He'd love hanging out with you. After we chat with your lawyer, we'll stop by the house and get him and his food. Just don't give him sugar or let him sleep on your bed. Mom spoils him when she babysits, and it takes me weeks to get him back in line."

Martin saw her shoulders relax. "Well, if you don't mind, that would be helpful. I'm afraid if I sleep I'm going to miss something."

"Oh, believe me, if there's something around your house, Bo will let you know. He probably wouldn't hear anything out near the creek, but at least you won't have to worry about someone getting into the house." He turned onto the highway that would take them into town. "Now will you tell me why you named your plant Candy?"

Martin learned a lot about Rhoda during that short trip, including what brought her to Peculiar. But as he parked the truck in front of Stine Law Office, he realized there was a lot more about her that he still had to learn. And, as he walked into the lobby with her, he realized he wanted to know everything.

One day at a time, he reminded himself. A relationship didn't happen immediately. Besides, maybe she didn't want a relationship. Or maybe she didn't like him. The thought froze him as she walked up to the reception desk. Then he shook it off. They were becoming friends, that was all.

But his attention followed her as the receptionist stood to show them into Jacob's office. He'd been expecting them.

Jacob greeted them at the door and motioned to the visitor chairs. "Come on in, Miss Grey, Martin. It's good to see the two of you today. Although I was a little surprised to get Martin's call this morning. I was under the impression that you, Miss Grey, weren't interested in selling your farm."

Rhoda sat in one of the chairs. "Please, call me Rhoda. You're correct, I'm not interested in selling. This concerns another issue.

I've been having trouble with someone vandalizing my farm. First it was a damaged sign, and then I found my irrigation ditch had been filled with dirt and had to be dug back out."

Mr. Stine's brow furrowed. "Those are troubling accusations, Miss Grey—Rhoda—but I think your time would be better spent talking with our sheriff. I can't handle a criminal issue, unless you're the one being charged, that is."

"Well, see, Mr. Stine, may I call you Jacob?" When he nodded, she continued. "I'm afraid that someone saw, well, I'm not sure how to put this."

Martin scooted up to the edge of his chair. "My foreman saw your car at the creek where our irrigation pump is located. What Rhoda is trying to ask is, why were you out there?"

"At the creek?" When both Martin and Rhoda nodded, he continued. "I was there because I needed to verify when Rhoda's irrigation times and days were. The ditch rider gave me a copy of your irrigation schedule along with an explanation on how to access the water. I had to meet him at the creek. He said he was too busy to come into town. I put the schedule on the desk at your uncle's house the day before you arrived."

Rhoda met Martin's gaze. He could tell she believed the lawyer.

Martin decided to take a chance with the truth. "Jacob, do you know anyone who might want Rhoda to give up and sell her farm?"

"That's what this is about? You think I was trying to get her to sell?" He chuckled. "I hate to throw a kink in your investigation, but I have no interest in buying a farm. My wife would kill me. She thinks I work too much as it is. If we lived on a farm, I'd be busy twenty-four seven."

Martin sank back into his chair. "Is there anyone else who might have a reason to sabotage Rhoda's farm?"

He steepled his fingers. "Besides you?" When Martin nodded, Jacob wrote something down on a sheet of paper and handed it to Rhoda. "There are a few people who expressed interest in purchasing the farm and asked me to pass the information on to you. Maybe your answer is on that list. I can't see any of these men breaking the law, but I've been wrong about people before."

Rhoda handed over the box of cookies. "These are for you, to thank you for all you did on the estate."

He took the box and opened the lid. Then he took a big whiff of the cookies. "It was my pleasure, but I appreciate the cookies. These are my favorite. My mother used to bake these when I was young. There's nothing like walking into a house with the smell of cookies baking to make you feel at home. I think you're going to be a delightful addition to our community, Rhoda."

As they walked out the door, Martin reached for the paper. "Do you mind?"

"How far do you want to get into what's my problem? You can walk away now, and no one would blame you. *I* wouldn't blame you." Rhoda paused outside the door. "If you go any further, it might change the way you think about people here."

"I said I'd help you, and I'm not changing my mind. Even if it's someone I know." He reached for the paper again. "Please."

She took a deep breath and handed him the paper. He unfolded it and read what Jacob had written down. There were three names on the list. Howard Mann, who was the president of the bank, Mayor Terrance Powers...and Chet Oaks.

Chapter Six

When Martin and Rhoda got back to the farmhouse, a note was stuck in the door. Rhoda went up the stairs to retrieve it. "I really hope I didn't miss a delivery of your mom's cookies. I can't stop eating them if they're in the house."

Martin followed her up to the porch. "Let's sit down with some tea and talk about these names. Just because they wanted to buy the place doesn't mean they'd do anything to get it, right?"

"True, but someone is trying to get me to sell. Or it's just kids being horrible. But they'd have to drive out here from town. No one close has kids, right?" Rhoda held the piece of paper in her hand as she unlocked the door. "Unless you can think of a third reason these things are happening."

"Believe me, I've been trying." He followed her into the house and then into the dining room.

She pointed to a chair. "Have a seat. I keep that side of the table clear so I have someplace to eat. Or entertain visitors."

"I'm not sure me hanging around and drinking your tea is considered entertaining." He picked up the note she'd dropped on the way to the kitchen. "Aren't you going to read this?"

"I'm parched," she called. "Let me get our tea, and then I'll read. I have some of your mom's oatmeal cookies left. Do you want one?"

"Sure, if you don't mind." He set the folded note back on the table. It wasn't his place to read something left for her. He glanced around the room. Fred had left the wallpaper his wife had put up right after their marriage. The room needed either new wallpaper or a coat of paint. That was one reason he loved his house. It was new, so he wasn't tired of the decisions he'd made. Now the decorating choices his mom had made, that was a different story.

Rhoda came back into the room and set a glass of tea in front of him. Then she set a plate of cookies on the table between then. She settled into a chair, took a long sip of her tea, and picked up the paper. "Your mom uses nice stationery. I'm surprised it doesn't have her initials on it."

"Oh, she has some like that. She uses it mostly for thank-you notes, I think." He picked up a cookie. "Mom's from the South, where manners are important. When I was a kid, I had to learn which fork to use when even though I've never gone anywhere that fancy. At least I'm prepared."

She laughed as she opened the note. A change fell over her face. "This isn't from your mom. But it looks like the same notepaper she uses."

She held out the page, and Martin took it. He read it aloud. "'For your own safety, you need to take the best offer for your land and leave Peculiar now or else something else might happen.'"

Martin met Rhoda's gaze. "This is my dad's handwriting."

Martin parked his truck in front of his parents' house. He'd already gone to his house to pick up Bo, and the dog jumped out of the truck bed as soon as Martin turned the engine off. Martin looked over at Rhoda. "Well, here we go."

Rhoda put a hand on his arm. "I don't think you should confront him. He's your father. I don't want my farm, or me, to get between the two of you."

"Rhoda, he wrote the note. If he's been doing this, or told someone to do it, he needs to stop. No matter what the reason." Martin squeezed her hand then reached for the door handle. "You don't have to go in with me."

"You're kidding, right? I'm going in. But you don't have to do this. I can talk to your father alone. Tell him I'm not interested in selling and ask him to tell whoever it is to stop harassing me." She stared at the house. "He can hate me, not you."

"If he's responsible for all this, I have to know. We've had our differences, but this isn't like him." He opened the truck door and climbed out. "I'll be fine. Just as soon as I know my dad isn't involved."

They walked up the front steps, and Bo found a place to curl up on the porch to wait for them. Martin opened the screen door and called out, "Mom, Dad? Where are you?"

"In the kitchen," Mom called back. "What are you doing here on a Thursday? Are you out of tea already?"

Martin moved through the house with Rhoda following him through the rooms and into the kitchen.

His mom sat at the table, writing in a journal. She smiled and stood as soon as she saw them. "Rhoda, isn't this a nice surprise? What are you doing here? And with Martin?"

Rhoda didn't meet Martin's gaze. "Martin's helping me with something."

"Mom, we need to talk to Dad. Where is he?" Martin pushed aside the implications of his mother's question and scanned the room then moved to the screen door, looking for his father.

"He's in town. He'll be back soon. He always spends Thursday mornings with those old geezers at Sally's Diner. Don't you remember?" Mom watched the two of them. "What's going on? Do you want to sit and talk? I can get you some tea, and I made your favorite brownies yesterday."

"I'm afraid we can't stay. I just need to ask him something. Have him call me when he gets back, okay?" Martin kissed his mother's cheek then turned to Rhoda. "Ready to go?"

"Yes. I've got a lot to do today if we're opening the U-pick stand on Saturday." She smiled at Mom, and Martin could see she was trying to act normal. "Nice to see you again. I'm going to start reading that book tonight."

"Great. I'm having the book club here at my house next Friday. I hope you can finish by then." Mom followed them as they walked back to the front door. "Martin, I'll give your message to your father as soon as he gets home. Are you sure you can't ask me?"

"It's just something I need to understand." Martin opened the screen door and held it for Rhoda. He snapped his fingers at Bo, who lay on the porch. "Come on, Bo, let's go."

Mom watched them as they got into the truck and left the driveway. Rhoda kept a smile on her face until they turned onto the road that would take them to her farm. Then she rubbed her arms. "I hate lying to your mother."

"We didn't lie. We just didn't tell her why I need to talk to Dad. If he wants to tell her, that's on him." Martin didn't say anything else, and in the next few minutes, they were at her house. Rhoda climbed out of the truck and followed him and Bo up the front steps. He held the door open for her. "Let's get Bo settled in the house, and then I'll get out of your hair."

"You're not a bother," Rhoda said. But Martin followed her gaze toward the unplanted garden. "Although I do need to finish up something, and the day's getting away from me. So where should I put Bo's food and water?"

They decided to set up a feeding station in the kitchen, and then Martin showed Bo where his food was located. The dog seemed to understand and lay down near it, watching them.

Martin chuckled. "He thinks I'm leaving him here and going on a trip. That's the pitiful look I get when I leave him with Mom."

"Maybe this isn't a good idea. I don't want him to be sad." Rhoda went over and scratched behind Bo's ears.

"Don't worry about it. He loves me, but he's accepted that sometimes he has to be somewhere else. This must be why Mom spoils him so bad. He makes her feel sorry for him. It's all an act." Martin smiled at Bo as the dog watched them talk.

"Well, it's working." Rhoda stood and moved to the sink. "I need to get my own dog, or you'll never get Bo back. He's growing on me."

"Dogs are a lot better pets than plants are. Just don't tell Candy I said that." Martin laughed and walked over to give Bo a last hug. "Keep him inside until I'm gone. Then use the lead to take him out for the first few times. I don't want him taking off to Mom and Dad's place."

"Okay, if you're sure." She followed Martin out of the house, shutting the door behind her. Martin was impressed that someone without a pet understood the connection between dog and master. As they stepped onto the porch, a truck came up the drive. "Isn't that your father?"

Martin's stomach cramped, but he ignored it. It was time to figure out what part, if any, his father had played in Rhoda's problems. Dad could still be unaware of all of this, except he hadn't just called, he'd come over to talk. Martin sat down in one of Rhoda's porch chairs. "Let's hear what he has to say."

It took a few minutes for Dad to settle, but when he did, he looked at Martin. "Son, I need to tell you something."

"Then say it." Martin exchanged glances with Rhoda. "We heard something today too. And you need to tell us why you wrote that note."

"It's not what you think. Or it's not as bad as you think. At least my part of the story." Dad ran a hand through his salt-and-pepper hair. "Okay, I'm just going to come out and say it. Rhoda, if you're not going to sell, you need to go to the courthouse and look up James Farm and any proposed developments."

"I'm not developing the farm," Rhoda protested. Martin squeezed her hand.

Dad leaned back and shrugged. "That's all I can say. I told him I wouldn't say anything, and I'm keeping that promise. But I don't like the way he's going about it. And I shouldn't have written the note. I just don't want you to get hurt in all this."

"This? As in someone is trying to develop the farm?" Martin asked.

Dad nodded. "That's all I can say. I don't want you to be unprepared."

"Dad, did you tell Jacob Stine that you wanted to buy the farm?" Martin wanted it all out on the table.

This time his dad looked confused. Martin took a deep breath and let the silence do its work.

"Yes, but that was months ago when Fred got sick. I asked him to let Fred know that we'd take James Farm and combine it with ours. I told him I'd give him a fair offer. Or his heirs." He stood and paced around the porch. Bo chuffed at him from the spot just inside the screen door where he'd sat to watch them. "What's Bo doing inside the house?"

"Visiting," Rhoda answered before Martin could say anything.

Martin leaned forward. "Then what happened? With Jacob and the offer."

Dad sank into a chair. "Your mother told me that you were probably Fred's heir, so I let it go. I wanted you to have the additional acreage for the farm. I know you're set on making this new process work."

"But he didn't make me the heir," Martin said. Martin knew his father. He decided not to push him. There was a reason he needed them to do their own research. And, for the first time in a long time, his father wasn't criticizing Martin's plans or actions. Martin saw the good intentions behind his visit. He stood and held out a hand to his father. "Why do you want us to go and look at any development plans?"

"Because someone else wants Rhoda to sell the property. And soon." Dad stood and put his ball cap on. "I can't tell you anything else without going back on my word."

"Thanks, Dad." Martin met Rhoda's gaze. "We'll go to the courthouse and figure this out. I just have one question. Is Rhoda safe?"

Martin's question made Rhoda shiver. She hadn't considered that someone might attack her, not just the farm. Now Martin had opened up the idea of her being in harm's way, and she couldn't shake it. She focused her gaze on Martin. "What do you mean?"

Martin reached over and took her hand. It made her feel a little stronger. "It's just a question. Dad, is this person going after Rhoda or her farm?"

Chet sputtered but then sighed. "Honestly, I'm not sure. Last week, I would have told you I trust this other person, but after what I heard yesterday, I'm not sure how far he'll go. That's why I left you the note."

"Thanks, Dad. I know this was hard, but Rhoda has a right to know." Martin met her gaze and squeezed her hand before dropping it again. "I'm not going to let anything happen to you."

For a moment, Rhoda couldn't catch her breath. Then she counted to ten. No one was going to chase her out of Peculiar. She was tired of being bullied. It was time to stand up and make them go away. Or at least try. "I believe you."

"I'm sure nothing's going to happen to you, Rhoda. Peculiar is a great town. We might have a few bad apples, but every place does. I'm sure this person was only talking." Chet brightened. "I have an idea. You need to get the town behind you. That way you're not so isolated. Are you going to the festival? It's a nice way for you to meet your neighbors."

"I'm going tomorrow night with Martin. I can't go on Saturday, because my U-pick shed is opening and I have to be there." Then she just kept talking. Maybe making this conversation somewhat normal would help her stop shaking. "Next week, I'll be open Wednesday, Friday, and Saturday. I'll adjust those dates as needed."

"You sound like you have a good plan for your farm. I hope you get to implement it." Chet stepped off the porch and got into his truck.

Rhoda looked over at Martin as his father drove away. "That sounded ominous."

"Yeah. Dad knows more than he's saying, that's for sure." He glanced at his watch. "We'd never get to the courthouse in time today. I'll come over first thing in the morning."

"I hate to keep you away from your farm so much. I could go by myself." She had to get the garden planted today. Especially since it looked like she was going to Kansas City in the morning.

He stood and leaned against the porch column. Rhoda wondered if he could see his father's truck on the road between the two farms. "I feel like I owe it to Fred to help you find out what's going on. I'm not going to let you go alone. I think that's part of their plan, to keep you guessing on who you can trust. We have to support each other."

Rhoda's heart sank a little. Of course there was a logical reason he was helping, and it wasn't because he was interested in a too-tall, too-shy girl from back East. He felt like he owed it to her uncle. She pasted on a smile and nodded. "Thanks for your friendship. It means a lot."

He studied her for a long time. "Friendship? You think that's what's going on between us? We're becoming friends?"

"I hope so." She glanced over at Bo, still sitting on the other side of the screen door watching them. From the look on the dog's face, bowl of popcorn. "Look, I'm just saying that I ...ss you trust me, since you left me Bo."

...emed to consider her answer, then he stood straight and nodded to his truck. "You're right. I've got work to do. I'll see you in the morning. Bo, you take good care of Rhoda now, you hear?"

A single bark made Rhoda laugh. "I think he knows his assignment."

"He's smart. Just listen to him and call me if he starts barking during the night." Martin waved and got into his truck.

As she watched him leave, she realized she was starving. She went inside and made a sandwich under Bo's watchful gaze. She sliced him a small sliver of cheese. He politely took the cheese from her fingers then licked his lips when he finished. She laughed at the look he gave her. "Clearly you want more, but I'm not sure about what dogs can eat. Let's leave it at that, and you can have some of your dog food if you're hungry while I eat my sandwich."

Bo went and lay down by his bowls to watch her eat. Then, as he figured out he wasn't getting anything else, he closed his eyes and fell asleep.

"Some watchdog," Rhoda teased.

Bo opened one eye and glared at her. Apparently, he didn't appreciate the comment.

"Fine, rest up, because I'm counting on you to be the first line of defense tonight if someone tries to tear up the farm." She watched as he closed his eyes again. She hoped he would be enough to scare away anyone with nefarious intentions. Rhoda had hoped that she'd just been overreacting. That kids had been responsible for the broken sign and maybe even the irrigation ditch. But if Chet Oaks felt

in Peculiar, Missouri

the need to warn her about some plot, she had to accept the reality of the situation. Someone wanted her to sell the farm and would go to great lengths to make that happen. But who?

That was a question she didn't have an answer for, so after she ate, she put her plate in the sink and went outside with Bo on his long lead. She tied it to a water trough by the garden area and got to work. She planted the peas first, hoping there would be enough warm days and cool nights left to get a bit of a crop before the full blast of summer heat hit the farm.

She and Bo had a long conversation about Martin while she planted. Bo was less than forthcoming on his master's intentions. But at least she had the time to work through what was going on with the two of them. He felt a duty to her because of her uncle. Nothing more, nothing less. Or if there was something more, it was friendship. Although she thought about the look on his face when she'd said they were friends. He'd been about to say something else. Hadn't he?

After the garden was planted, Rhoda stood and dusted dirt off her knees. She woke Bo from his nap—he'd stopped listening a while ago—and they went back to the house. It was nice having someone that she could talk to, even if it was a dog.

And having Bo around gave her someone to take care of besides herself. She put a casserole in the oven to heat and took a book to the porch to read. Her brain was filled with what-ifs, and spending some time reading always helped her thoughts slow down a little. Sometimes she even found an answer. As she sat on the porch watching the sun slowly set, she wondered if April had replaced her at the insurance company yet. She wouldn't need the job if she sold James

Farm, but if she had to go back to Baltimore, she needed something to do.

She laid the book down and went over to the railing to take in the darkening evening. At the apartment, all her windows faced east or north, so sunsets had to be watched from the rooftop. It had been a while since she'd taken the time to be still and listen. She closed her eyes and gave a quick prayer of thanks. No matter what happened, this was a perfect moment. And she was going to enjoy it for everything it gave her.

Later that night, a noise woke her from a restless sleep. Bo jumped off the bed where he'd been lying and took off downstairs. She switched on the flashlight she'd put on her nightstand and glanced out her window. A car sat almost out of sight. If she had gone downstairs before glancing out the window, she never would have seen it. Or if it hadn't been a full moon. As it was, she was able to see a man carrying a bag and running down her driveway toward the car. Something dropped out of the bag, but the shadowy figure kept running.

She waited and watched. Bo stopped barking and came back upstairs. She reached down and stroked his head. "Good dog. You scared him away. You're such a good boy."

Bo leaned on her leg, loving the attention.

After she heard the car start and then saw its lights disappear down the road, she stepped away from the window and tightened the belt on her robe. She wished she'd been able to see the car clearly. Maybe a description or even a license plate. Now that would have been helpful.

She tucked the flashlight into her pocket and turned on her bedroom light. Putting on her slippers, she addressed Bo. "Want to see what the bad man dropped?"

Bo barked.

The dog was attentive. She didn't know if that was natural for him, or if Martin had trained him well. They made their way downstairs, and she grabbed her camera from the table by the door. When they reached the porch, she turned on the flashlight. Moths fluttered around the porch light, and as she reached the yard, a swarm of gnats followed her. She dropped the angle of the light so she wouldn't have to walk through the bugs and headed down the driveway.

An owl hooted in the darkness. She was just about to give up when she saw it—a package of salt sitting on the side of the driveway. She focused the light on the package. Depending on how many boxes of salt he'd brought, her midnight caller could have poisoned most of her crop just by dumping the salt into the irrigation ditch that Steve had set up to water the front field.

The box was off the path enough that she didn't think Martin or Steve would drive over it in the morning. She fiddled with her Polaroid camera. She'd replaced the flashcube before she'd gone to bed just in case she needed to use it. She set the flashlight on the ground, illuminating the area, then aimed the camera lens at the packet.

The first picture was fuzzy, so she took a second one. When that picture developed, it clearly showed the salt packet. She glanced over at Bo, who watched her.

"Time to go to bed. I don't think we'll be bothered again tonight." She gathered the camera and the two photos and turned off the flashlight. Her eyes had become accustomed to the low light from the moon.

After locking the front door behind her, she stared out the window at the spot where the salt had fallen. What was going on around here? She set everything on the table and headed back upstairs. Maybe she'd sleep now. She could figure out the puzzle tomorrow when Martin came over.

Chapter Seven

Rhoda and Bo were sitting on the porch when Martin drove up the driveway the next morning. She could see by the look on his face that he realized something had happened. He'd probably hoped that with Bo around she'd be able to get some sleep. Instead, she'd been up most of the night. He parked the truck, and Rhoda stepped off the porch to greet him.

He got out of the truck and shut the door, "Everything okay?"

"Actually, no. Come see this." Rhoda marched down the driveway and stopped where the salt box was.

Standing next to her, he stared at the box. "That's canning salt. The kind my mother uses for pickling. What happened? Why is it out here?"

"Bo woke me about midnight, and when he went downstairs to bark at the front door, I stayed at the bedroom window and watched. The moon was bright last night. Anyway, Bo scared off someone carrying a large bag. When he got here, this box fell out of it. He could have ruined my entire bottom strawberry field if Bo hadn't scared him off. I took a picture of the box. I know it doesn't show us who did this, but maybe we could ask at the grocery store and see if anyone bought this brand of salt recently. And they were driving a car. Not a truck."

"Whoever did this probably bought the salt in Kansas City, not at Peculiar General. But we can ask Arnold. He's the owner." He rubbed Bo's head as he glanced around the farmyard. "Who's a good dog? I knew you needed him. Did you get any sleep at all?"

"Not much," Rhoda admitted. She handed him a paper bag. "I guess we should keep the salt just in case. It's evidence, right? I don't think calling the police would do any good right now."

"I'm afraid you're right. But sure, let's put this aside. Maybe we can find more clues to add to it." Martin picked up the box using two fingers and slipped it into the paper bag as she held it open. "We should tape this or staple it."

"I have tape in my office." She folded the top of the bag down. "Let me get this put away, and then I'll be ready to run to the courthouse."

"We could do that next week." He followed as she headed to the house.

She turned to meet his gaze. "I need to get my life back. I need to find out who's doing this."

"I think we should leave Bo here. I'll grab his long lead, and we'll put him on the porch. Maybe just seeing him will keep any vandals from stopping by while we're gone." He followed her into the house. "I'll get his food and water."

"I'll let Steve know he's here, and he can check on him before we get back. I hate to leave Bo alone." She watched Martin head to the kitchen as she paused at the office doorway.

When she joined him in the kitchen, he'd gathered everything Bo needed. "He'll be fine on the porch. He likes hanging out and watching. When I'm working on the farm, he usually heads over to Mom's for a midday treat."

"He knows she's a soft touch." Rhoda glanced around the kitchen and double-checked the lock on the back door.

"We're going to find out who's doing this, I promise," Martin said as he watched her move around the kitchen.

She nodded and set a dishrag by the sink. "I know. I'm finally settling in. I don't want someone to force me out."

"That's not going to happen. Let's go find out what my dad was trying to tell us yesterday." Martin took Bo's stuff outside. She left him to set up Bo's feeding station as well as his favorite blanket in a spot where he'd have shade most of the day. She went to look for Steve to let him know they were leaving and to ask him to check on Bo once in a while.

A few minutes later she returned. "We should be back before the deck gets too sunny."

They got into the truck and headed to the highway that would take them to Kansas City. She watched the scenery and leaned out to catch the air.

He chuckled from the other side of the cab. "Is it bad to say you remind me of Bo?"

Rhoda leaned back into the truck and away from the window and stared at him. "I guess not, especially since you won't live long enough to regret it."

"I don't mean it in a bad way. You're just so in the moment. You're amazing." He reached over and squeezed her hand. "You have all these bad things happening, and you can still find enjoyment in watching the river."

"So you're not saying I look like a dog."

Her words must have surprised him, because he turned his head sharply and stared at her. "No. Not even close. You're beautiful."

What? "I'm not beautiful."

"Why on earth would you say that?" He slowed the truck down a bit and met her gaze in the mirror.

"I'm plain. I always have been. Plain Grey. That was my nickname in school." Her cheeks burned as she remembered the embarrassment she'd felt.

"Kids are idiots. You're beautiful. Maybe you were in an awkward stage at school, but if they could see you now, no one would call you Plain Grey." He turned onto the road that would take them to the courthouse. "You should have seen my ears in high school. I got a few Dumbo references, but then they realized I was a very good quarterback. So they stopped calling me names or, technically, they kept calling me names, just had a smile when they did. To show they were teasing. I think you need to forget the past and focus on what you're good at. That's where your true beauty shines. Like with plants. You light up when you talk about the farm and what you want to do."

She didn't say much for a while as he navigated the streets and finally parked the truck. Before he could get out, she touched his arm. "Thank you for saying that. I've been holding on to that teasing for way too long."

He squeezed her fingers. "I only pointed out the truth. You are beautiful. And you should know it."

"I like hanging out with you." Rhoda opened her door and got out of the truck. When he met her on the sidewalk, she smiled at him. "You make me feel special."

He took her arm as they walked up the stairs of the courthouse. "You are special. And I'll keep telling you that until you believe it."

in Peculiar, Missouri

Martin leaned on the counter as Rhoda chatted with the clerk. She had a good, believable story, and the clerk gave her everything they needed. Rhoda had a way with people. Much better than his business-focused approach. He hadn't even noticed the picture of the baby on the clerk's desk behind the counter. Rhoda had cooed over the child, winning the new mother to her cause quickly.

"So, can you show me the plat of James Farm? Without being able to talk to my uncle before he died, I guess I might have to have a survey done of the property so I know where my borders are. I'd hate to plant my neighbor's field." Rhoda gave the street address for the farm to the clerk.

"I can, but according to this, there was a survey done just a few weeks ago. Let me pull it up, and we can see if your uncle asked for it before he died." She pulled out another plat book and then frowned. "It wasn't your uncle who ordered the survey. It was the town of Peculiar."

"The town ordered it?" Martin leaned forward, trying to see the book on the other side. "Is that normal in a resident's death?"

The clerk, Jenny was her name, shook her head. "This is the first time I've seen a survey ordered by a town. Usually it's a neighborhood dispute or..." She leaned closer to the survey to check out some writing. She tapped a finger on the notation. "Or it's someone who wants to know what they're buying. Like when they're trying to put in a new road."

Martin met Rhoda's gaze. He felt his body tighten, but he tried to keep looking casual. "A road?"

"Yeah, like a highway." Jenny called back to a woman on a typewriter. "Clara, is there any road construction around Peculiar going on or in the planning stages?"

Clara didn't look up. "The county is putting in a new highway so traffic doesn't have to run directly through Kansas City. Remember, we talked about it at the last staff meeting? They've been putting in easements for the land."

"Do you have a proposed survey or map of the new road?" Martin couldn't act casual anymore. This was the *why* behind the weird stuff going on at James Farm. And if they were going after Rhoda's place, they might go after Nate's family farm too. He took a breath. Or Oaks Farm. Would his dad sell off part of their farm for a quick retirement payout? And even if he didn't, what would a highway do to the farm? He pushed the questions away as Jenny handed him a copy of the map and the packet the developer had put together for community involvement.

"Just call that number." Jenny pointed to a number on top of the first fact sheet. "They'll be able to answer your questions about the proposal."

"One more question." Rhoda took the folder from Martin and tucked it into her purse. "Has the land been purchased by the state yet? I don't know if my uncle handled this and I should be looking for a contract in his mess of an office, or if this is still just in the proposal stage."

Clara came up from the back desk. "The project is still in the process of being approved. There's a community meeting scheduled on the books. That folder has a list of the next steps, depending on if you're for the development or not. But I don't think you're going to be getting a check anytime soon. Even though the project is almost out of the community-input stage, the funding process takes forever."

As they walked out of the courthouse, Martin took Rhoda's arm and moved her out of the way of several men in suits heading upstairs. He pulled her aside after they got to the sidewalk. "You look shell-shocked. Are you okay?"

"It's just been a lot these last few weeks. First, Uncle Fred, who I don't remember, dies and leaves me the farm. Then the vandalism and the offers to sell. Now I find out they want to build a road through my strawberry patch?" She started laughing. "What's next? Locusts? Fire? Flood? Famine?"

He saw a bench to the side of the building. He led her over and they sat. "It's not that bad. I know you've been through a lot of changes lately. We'll figure this out."

Rhoda leaned into his shoulder and appeared to be trying to control her giggles. Finally, she took a deep breath and sat up straight. She adjusted her jacket and ran her hands over her hair, smoothing down the tight braid. She was soothing herself, he realized. He kept his hands by his side, even though he wanted to put his arms around her and comfort her. It wasn't his place. Not yet anyway.

Finally, she took another breath and pulled the folder out of her purse. A look of determination set her features, and a fire burned in her eyes. "Thank you for the use of your shoulder. I can't believe I fell apart like that. It's not like me."

"You're welcome. But you've been through a lot. It's okay to feel overwhelmed. How can I help?"

"You've done a lot already. I would like to keep Bo for a few days. Now that we've found out why someone wants me to tuck my tail between my legs and leave Peculiar, we need to find out who's behind these shenanigans." She tapped the folder. "Tonight, when we go to the festival, we need to talk to as many people as possible. I can say it's to build business for the U-pick grand opening tomorrow. You need to watch and see if anyone reacts funny to what I say."

"Like laughing maniacally to himself?" Martin wasn't sure it would be that easy to spot a villain.

She tucked the folder away, stood, and walked toward his truck. "I didn't say it was going to be easy. But it might be fun."

He followed her to the truck, wondering what he'd gotten himself into. A smile tugged at his lips. Rhoda was right about one thing. This situation was interesting at least. For a long time, the only thing he'd thought about was the farm and getting more yield from the crops. Oh, and to prove his father wrong. Now, he thought about a lot of things—most importantly, keeping Miss Rhoda Grey here in town and safe. She was a force of nature and, as he started the truck, he knew his life would be duller without her around.

"We haven't talked about the other two names on the list. Howard Mann and Terrance Powers." He turned the truck onto the highway as he talked. "Have either of them reached out to you?"

She told him about the visit from the mayor. "Mr. Powers, or Mayor Powers, I should say, would have known about the highway, right? He said he wanted the farm as a retirement place. I guess selling it off for development would put money in his pocket."

"True, but he is getting older. I heard Dad say that his wife doesn't want him to run in the next election. She wants them to slow down."

Rhoda nodded. "That's what he told me too. Said she wanted to get him moving and not behind a desk all the time."

"It sounds logical. What about the banker, Howard Mann? Has he made an offer?" They were close to being back on her farm.

"I met him when I went to transfer the farm accounts to my name. Just a quick 'welcome to Peculiar.' Nothing that felt off." Rhoda stared out the window. "I hate having to dissect every conversation to see if there's a lie in the middle. I want to trust everyone."

"You would be able to in a perfect world," Martin said. "Of course, I always thought Peculiar was that perfect world."

When they got to her farm, Martin hung around a bit at the house, spending some time with Bo until it got obvious Rhoda was too busy to sit and chat. "I'll pick you up at five. The festival opens then, and we'll eat first so we can catch the early birds who'll be in the food tent and leaving as soon as they're done." He paused at the truck. "I think you're going to be busy tomorrow, even if you just have people stopping in to see what you're doing."

"I'm going to have Steve pick a few quarts so we'll have some for people who don't want to pick their own." She rubbed Bo's head. "Sorry about stealing your dog."

"You didn't steal him. He's on loan." He waved at her and got into his truck. When he reached Oaks Farm, Nate was at the barn, watching for him. He turned off the engine and headed over to see what was going on. "Everything okay?"

"We're all planted, watered, and just waiting for a round of cultivating next week. I brought on a few extra hands to clean out the barn and get us ready for harvest, but I'm thinking we should let them off for the weekend. A lot of them want to go to the festival."

Nate handed Martin the checklist he'd made up with what needed to be done the next few days. "Do you agree? I can come by and check on everything if you need me."

Martin shook his head. "No, you spend the weekend finishing up over at your place. How are things going?"

"I'm really sorry I didn't tell you about borrowing the tractor." Nate kicked at a lump of dirt on the ground. "I should have trusted you."

"Yes, you should have. But that's water under the bridge." He remembered that the Jones farm had been in the possible road area too. "Hey, have you heard anything about the county building a new road out here?"

Nate frowned, shaking his head. "No, but last month I got a weird offer from someone wanting to buy the farm. The guy said he'd call back in a few weeks, but he never did. I guess he bought somewhere else."

Martin wondered if the mystery man had called Nate before Fred James had died and put Rhoda's place in play. "Just keep an eye out. James Farm has been having some issues with someone trying to harm the crops. I'd hate to have that spill over to your place or mine."

"So that's why you don't have Bo today? He's babysitting?" Nate grinned.

"You could say that." He slapped Nate on the back and headed into the shed. "Are you going to the festival tonight?"

Chapter Eight

When she heard the truck pull up the gravel drive, Rhoda looked at the clock. It was four. Not five. Martin was an hour early. She slipped on her shoes and headed downstairs. She had a sundress on, but her hair was still wet and down around her shoulders. She opened the door and was surprised to see Jacob Stine standing on the porch. "Jacob, I wasn't expecting you."

He held out an envelope. "I'm sorry to disturb you. I closed out Mr. James's estate file today and found this letter for you. He gave it to me a couple of months ago, and I forgot about it. Better late than never, right?"

She took the envelope and looked at her name on the front. "He wrote this to me?"

"Yes. He said he wanted you to know why he left you the farm." Jacob nodded to Candy, Rhoda's sole tomato plant that had survived the Baltimore disaster as well as the trip across the country. "He loved plants as much as it seems you do. He was always talking about the farm and the new things he was trying. I saw your U-Pick sign on the road. My wife and I will be here early tomorrow to purchase a few quarts. She's really excited about coming by."

"Well, you might be my first and only customers." Rhoda tried not to be rude and stare at the envelope in her hands. But she really wanted to rip it open and read what this long-lost relative had to say to her. Or did she? Her mother hadn't talked a lot about her family or where she'd come from. Mostly she'd talked about plants and their garden. The rest of her thoughts, she'd kept close. Rhoda had given up trying to find out about her mom's history, hoping that in time her mother would feel comfortable answering her questions. Then her parents had been killed. And Rhoda had been alone. At least that's what she'd thought. She tuned back in to what Jacob was saying.

"Your little experiment is the talk of the town. Everyone's excited to support you and James Farm. You're a breath of fresh air around here." He headed down the steps. "I'll see you at the festival tonight?"

"I'll be there." Rhoda waved and then noticed Bo sitting by her feet. Not growling, not talking, just watching out for her. She rubbed his head as Jacob left. "You're a great guard dog, aren't you? Silent but watchful."

He looked up at her, and she could have sworn he grinned. At least in doggy language. She scratched his ears, went back inside, and glanced at the clock on the wall. No time to get lost in memories right now. She set the letter on the desk in her office. "I'll read you as soon as I get back from the town festival, I promise."

Now, she had to hurry and finish getting ready for...her ride? Her date? She decided to just call him by his name. *Martin* would be here in less than thirty minutes.

Bo lay down by the front door, and she paused in the middle of the stairway. She felt at home here. For the first time since she'd closed up her parents' house after the sale, she had a place to not just sleep but to live. This was home. And no one, no highway, was going to drive her off her land. Not today, not ever.

Martin arrived exactly on time, and she wondered if he'd been sitting on the side of the road, waiting for the hands on his watch to read five o'clock. She was outside on the porch, sitting with Bo. She'd filled his water dish and his food dish and had the long lead next to her. She would ask Martin if he wanted Bo left inside or outside. He'd been a good boy and hadn't had any accidents, so she wasn't worried about leaving him in the house by himself. She just wanted him to be happy.

She rubbed his head again, laughing at her thoughts. Before, all she had to worry about was her potted plants. Now, she had a loaner dog. She was going to have to change that soon and let Martin take Bo home.

"You seem happy." Martin came up the steps, a bundle of daisies in his hand. "These are for you."

"When did you have time to buy me flowers?" She took them from him and stood. "I've got the perfect vase for these. It's under the kitchen sink."

"I guess that's where I'd put a vase if I had one." He followed her inside, holding the door for Bo. "My mom taught me to never come to a first date empty-handed."

She almost stumbled at the word *date*, but he'd said it, not her. She smiled to herself as she rinsed and filled the vase with water then arranged the flowers. She'd never received flowers on a date before. Actually, she'd never gotten flowers before ever. "They're beautiful, thank you."

"You're welcome. I hoped you would like them. I could have brought you roses, but you have rosebushes here. In fact, you have the same rosebushes I do, since my plants are cuttings off your uncle's plants."

When she turned around with the flowers, she saw him leaning against the doorway, watching her. "Well, they're perfect. I'll keep them right here on the kitchen table. You know I've taken over the dining room table with all my papers and plans."

"Mom says flowers always make a house a home." He pointed to Bo's dog dishes by the back door. "So, are we leaving him in or out? I can move those to the front porch if you need me to."

"I thought I'd leave it up to you where we left him. He's been great, so he can stay in if you don't want him on a lead while we're gone." She set the vase on the table.

"I'd shut off the bedrooms if you don't want him sleeping on the beds. It's better if you limit his access while he's alone. He's curious." Martin laughed as Bo looked up at him as if to say, *Are you talking about me?*

"Then let's leave him inside. No one is going to get in the house with him on guard." She checked the lock on the kitchen door and led the way through the dining room. "I'll go grab a shawl and my purse."

"Bo and I will wait here." He paused at the dining room table. "Is it okay if I look at your crop plans?"

"Crop plans?" She glanced back at the table. "Oh, my future farm dreams? I guess I need to start talking in farm terms. That's fine. Maybe you can look at my fruit tree plan over by the creek. I'm not sure if I'm under- or overplanting there."

"Sure." He sat down where she'd been earlier that day and moved a paper closer.

She watched him for a moment and realized they were two of a kind. Both of them could get lost in planning for the future. *For the crop yields*, she corrected. Maybe Uncle Fred had some farming books around so she could read up on the terminology. She knew plants and gardening, but farming? It was more deliberate and at a much larger, and more expensive, level. She had a lot to learn.

As she headed upstairs, she thought about the letter from Uncle James. "I hope you didn't place too much trust in me," she whispered. "I hope I won't make you sorry you left me the farm."

Martin laid the last paper down. He hadn't had much time to review the plans, but they were good. Outstanding, if you considered Rhoda had never planned out a farm before. She was using every square foot of the land for appropriate crops. He would have probably replaced all the strawberry fields with corn, but that was his crop, not hers. She had fruit all over. And her "garden" would be large enough to supply her needs and have enough left over to stock the roadside stand and make some money on the extra.

If they could only figure out who wanted her gone. He thought about the people he knew from Peculiar. They were nice. They helped each other. And yet, the prospect of making money from the development around a highway had turned somebody into a villain. One that was trying to run Rhoda off the property she was trying to make her home.

His dad had to know who was doing this. He'd been hesitant to tell them about the highway. But his conscience had gotten the better of him. Maybe because Mom liked Rhoda. Maybe because his dad did. But either way, Martin was going to have a heart-to-heart with his dad tomorrow and, hopefully, get the name of the troublemaker.

She stood in the doorway, watching him. He smiled when he saw her. "Ready to go?"

"Yes." She didn't move. "What do you think? A good start? You look pensive. You can tell me the truth. I'm a big girl."

"I think you've done an amazing job. Would I have made different choices? Maybe. Okay, probably. But that's Oaks Farm, not James Farm. If you focus on fruits, you'll carve out a niche that no one else has in the area." He carefully moved the papers into a neat pile. "You're a natural with this. I went to college and got a degree in agriculture, and you worked in an office. Did you have any schooling in farming techniques?"

A smile crossed her lips. "I was just thinking that I needed to do some reading in the subject. My formal education is in secretarial skills. I'm excellent at accounting and verifying claims. But I don't know anything about crop rotation."

"You'll figure it out. I'll bring over my textbooks. I've still got them. They fill up some of the bookshelves in my den." He stood and moved the chair back under the table. "Let's go have some fun and forget about everything else."

"If it were only that easy." But she smiled and took his offered arm. "So you have a den? How big is that house you built?"

"Bo, stay." He opened the door for her and then waited while she locked it. "Technically, the plans called it a three-bedroom house. But since it's just me, I made one of the bedrooms into a den. I couldn't see having two guest rooms. That's a roommate disaster waiting to happen. I like living alone."

They chatted about their respective houses and the plans they had to remodel or landscape the flower beds. Mostly Rhoda chatted and he listened, but it was nice to hear that she was starting to plan her life based on staying in Peculiar. As they pulled up to the fairgrounds, she grew quiet. He looked over and saw her hands clasped tightly together in her lap. "It'll be fine. You'll meet a lot of people, and they'll love you. We're a friendly group."

"Except for the guy who wants to run me off my farm." She met his gaze. "I hate looking at everyone like they're a suspect."

"Then let's figure it out, and after we talk to him, or her, we'll know who the enemy is." He parked and turned off the engine. "Now, let's go eat. They have the best hamburgers here. I can't replicate them at home. Maybe you can tell me what I'm doing wrong."

She met him on the other side of the truck, and he watched as she ran her hand down the skirt of her flower-covered sundress. She was still nervous. She met his gaze. "I'm thinking if you're looking at me for cooking advice, we're both in trouble. I cook the way my mom always did. A lot of veggies mixed together. In Baltimore, canned vegetables were cheaper, but I always tried to buy as much fresh produce as possible. It just tastes better."

"I'm not going to argue with you there. Besides, Mom still supplies most of the meals I have at home. I've told her I can make it without her feeding me, but she thinks I'll starve without her." He took her arm, and they strolled toward the festival and the food tent. "I'm sure she's probably cooking tonight. She volunteers for at least one night each festival."

"Then we're in for a treat. Your mom's food is out of this world. At least what I've tasted." She smiled at him, and his heart skipped a beat.

He blinked, pushing the questions behind him. First date, and they had an agenda. He couldn't be mooning over her blue eyes all night. He'd have to save that for after he'd dropped her at home and he was alone. He didn't want to scare her off.

Jacob Stine saw them walk in and waved them over to a table. "About time you two showed up. Angelia, this is the woman I've been telling you about, Rhoda Grey."

Angelia set the spoon down that she'd been using to feed a chubby-faced baby some sort of puree. "Rhoda, we're so excited to come out tomorrow morning. I'm going to make some strawberry baby food with what we pick. Although, I do have a question. Do you use pesticides? I've been reading some concerning facts."

"I think it's smart to read up on what you're feeding your family and especially that adorable child. No, my fields are pesticide free." Rhoda shot Martin a look. "I wish all of our local farms could say that."

"Now look, Angelia, you're trying to start a fight between these two." Jacob winked at Martin. "I'm sure you have a different perspective, Martin. Anyway, I bet you're hungry. We'll let you go and see you tomorrow."

Martin took Rhoda's arm, and they aimed toward the table where they would pay for their meals. "If we stop and chat with everyone, we're never going to eat. People will come to us, I promise. And there's nothing wrong with using modern methods in your farming techniques."

Rhoda pointed back at Angelia, who was feeding the baby again. "Tell that to a new mother who just wants the best for her baby. I've done a lot of reading on pesticide use and our food chain."

"Then let's talk about this later, not here. We need to find your nemesis, not get in a fight about our farming processes." He pulled out his wallet and paid the woman at the table for their meals. He introduced Rhoda to the woman and then grabbed a tray and handed it to her. "You can have two entrees, three sides, and a dessert."

"You'll have to roll me out of here if I eat all that." She paused at the fried chicken. "Okay, I have to have some of that."

By the time they went through the line, they each had different entrees, sides, and desserts with a plan to share so Rhoda could taste almost everything. Martin grabbed two glasses of sweet tea and set them on the table before sitting down. "I warned you that Mom's cooking tonight. Everything's going to be great."

"At least we'll spend the rest of the evening walking around and talking to people, so maybe I won't be too full to sleep tonight." She pointed to a table where a man sat eating alone. "I know him. That's Mayor Powers, right?"

"Terrance. It is. He's the one who came to the house?"

Rhoda took a sip of her tea. "Yes. But he doesn't look like a villain."

"Sometimes you can't tell the good guys from the bad guys from their looks." Martin turned and watched the mayor. Terrance waved then set his fork down and walked over to where they sat.

"Good evening, Martin, Rhoda. I'm happy to see you out and away from the farms. You farmers work too hard." Terrance reached out to shake hands with Martin.

"Sunup to sundown hours, that's for sure. Not banker's hours." Martin stood to shake Terrance's hand. "I hear you've been out campaigning already."

Terrance frowned. "Now, where would you have heard that?"

"Oh, I just meant that Rhoda mentioned you stopped by her farm." Martin nodded at Rhoda.

"Oh yes, I'm always excited when a possible new voter comes into the area. Of course, I assumed that she'd be selling and moving on soon." He stared at Rhoda. "And I was told I was incorrect."

"I'm not sure where you got that idea in the first place." Rhoda kept her eye contact steady. "I'm enjoying my time here in Peculiar. I've got a grand opening tomorrow for the U-pick season. I hope your wife will come and buy her strawberries from James Farm."

"My wife doesn't put up jam or can. In fact, she's at her sister's this week, so I'm sorry we won't be buying from your roadside stand. At least not tomorrow." He tapped the table. "I need to go. I'm doing an opening speech for the festival soon."

Martin watched as the mayor returned to his table then took his barely touched plate to the trash can and exited the tent.

Martin exchanged a look with Rhoda. "That was weird."

"He was a lot nicer when he stopped by the house. I guess he realized I was serious." Rhoda put her questions about the mayor aside and pointed to the scalloped potatoes. "These are amazing."

As they enjoyed their dinner, more people came up to their table to meet Rhoda. A lot of them told her they'd be at the U-pick grand opening the next day. By the time they'd finished eating, he felt like most of the town of Peculiar had stopped by to either meet Rhoda or tell her what a great idea her farm was going to be. Several mentioned how much her late uncle would be missed.

Martin stood and got two more iced teas as a little girl dressed in a Brownie uniform came by to clear their plates off the table.

When he returned, he handed Rhoda a napkin and her glass of tea. "Are you okay? I told you we'd be flooded with visitors."

She nodded. "Everyone's so nice."

He watched her look around the tent. "We have good neighbors."

"They don't question me about working the farm. They don't ask how tall I am. They just invite me to another book club or coffee with a knitting group, and everyone seems to want to come out and buy my strawberries." She shook her head. "I've talked to more people here in one night than I did all the years I lived in Baltimore. I rode the bus with the same people for more than two years and never made a friend. People were so busy with their own lives."

"Peculiar's the best of small-town America. We care about each other." He glanced around the tent. "Except we aren't any closer to finding out who wants your farm. I still think we should keep both the mayor and Howard on our watch list."

Rhoda sipped her tea. "We need to ask about the salt. Who runs the general store? Have we met them yet?"

"Arnold Ness. He hasn't come by, but he might be in the back, cooking with Mom. Do you want to go see?"

Rhoda finished her tea and stood. "Hopefully he'll remember who bought a huge amount of salt recently. We need to find this guy soon. I've got customers depending on me."

Martin smiled and led her to the back of the tent where the kitchen was located. He liked this confident Rhoda. Especially when she talked about staying here in Peculiar. He wouldn't say he was invested in her staying, but he was looking forward to it.

Chapter Nine

The kitchen for the festival was located in a shed near the back of the tent. Several stoves lined the walls as well as sinks, and in the middle of the area sat a long table. It met up with another table to make a T shape by the entrance. Savannah Oaks stood at the table like a military captain and waved them over to where she was pushing a metal tub filled with macaroni and cheese to a waiting server. "Now watch out, that's hot." She turned to Martin and Rhoda. "What are the two of you doing in here? You should go through the exhibit hall. If you do, check and see if they've awarded ribbons yet. I've got a few entries I'm hopeful will at least place this year. I've been working on that banana bread for months to get it right."

"We'll do that." Martin winked at Rhoda then turned back to his mother. "I'm sure you'll take home several blue ribbons. You always do."

Savannah shook her head. "That's mostly at the fall festival. I always seem to place second to Maddy Evans at this one."

"I'm sure you'll do great. We, I mean, I, am wondering if Arnold Ness is here. I've got a quick question." As Martin spoke, Rhoda looked around the room. Most of the occupants were women, but there was one man.

"Arnold, come over here and meet our newest Peculiar resident. She just took over running James Farm," Savannah called out.

in Peculiar, Missouri

The short, balding man stepped away from the fryer and motioned for someone to take his place. Then he wiped the sweat off his forehead with a towel and walked over to them. "Miss Grey? I've been meaning to get out to your farm and chat with you about purchasing some of your strawberries for my store. I'd love to work out a deal, but with the festival, I've been busy, I'm afraid."

"Oh, that would be lovely." Rhoda glanced over at Martin. "I know this isn't the time to chat, but I have an odd question for you."

"I'm all about the odd." The man smiled and showed a gold tooth. "I live in Peculiar."

Rhoda laughed at his joke and then took a breath. "Has anyone come into your store recently to buy a lot of salt?"

He blinked at her then looked at Martin.

Great, now he thinks I'm an idiot. Rhoda hurried to add, "Like I said, I know it's a strange question."

"Actually, I was just wondering how you knew. The question is oddly specific." He shifted from one foot to the next. "Yes, Terrance Powers came in on Monday and cleaned me out of salt. He said his wife was doing some pickling. I had to send my helper into Kansas City to restock the store."

Martin locked gazes with Rhoda. "He bought canning salt?"

"Arnold, can you check this chicken? I think it's burning," a voice called.

"Yes, canning salt. Sorry, I've got to go." He hurried back to the fryer, calling out as he went, "Margie, I told you to watch the fryer."

Savannah wiped her hands on her apron as she studied them. "Why are you interested in salt?"

"Long story. Do you know what time the mayor's opening the festival and where?" Rhoda asked her.

"Oh, that's already done. The opening ceremonies took place right at five. That's why we're so swamped here at the food tent. Everyone wants to eat before they go check out the rest of the festival." Savannah pointed to the table as someone brought a pan of hamburgers from the staging table. "Set those there. Sorry, kids, I've got to get this food out."

As they moved out of the shed and onto the gravel walkway leading to the carnival site, Rhoda gasped and grabbed Martin's arm. "He was lying about the opening ceremonies. He must be heading to my place. We need to leave now."

Martin glanced around the tents with the local clubs and public services lining the walkway. He pointed to one at the center of the festival. "We need to make a stop first."

By the time they got back to the farm, it was quiet. Steve was just pulling out of the driveway, and Martin stopped the truck next to him so they could talk. "Any issues?"

"No. I saw a car slow down out here, but I was at the shed doing the final setup for tomorrow morning. I think they saw me and kept going. You don't think we're going to have problems tonight, do you?" He looked past Martin and focused on Rhoda.

"I'm sure it'll be fine," Rhoda said. She was concerned, but she didn't want to worry Steve. "Go home. I'll see you first thing in the morning. From what people told me tonight, we're going to be busy."

Steve grinned. "Now that's what I like to hear. I'm meeting Tina at the festival to grab dinner."

in Peculiar, Missouri

He drove off, and Martin continued to the house. He turned off the engine, and they went inside. He was letting Bo out when Rhoda's phone rang.

Rhoda answered the call. She waved at Martin to continue taking care of Bo. "Hello?"

"Hello, Miss Grey," Mayor Powers said. "Are you too busy for a visit?"

"No, I'm not busy. Why?"

"I'd like to come over and make you a better offer on the farm."

"I've already told you I'm not interested in selling."

"Look, I think you should hear what I'm going to say. It's a lot of money."

"I'm home, so come by when you want." She said goodbye and hung up.

When Martin came back inside, she was sitting at the table. "Well?"

"The mayor is coming by now. He wants to make me a better offer on the farm." Rhoda took her sweater off the dining room chair where she'd hung it and put it on. She was freezing. "I guess he's done playing games with this."

He nodded to the kitchen. "Go make some coffee, and I'll get everything ready."

By the time Mayor Powers pulled his car into the driveway, Rhoda was sitting alone on the porch. Bo lay by her side. The mayor walked up the steps. "Look, I don't want any trouble. I just think you should do the right thing and sell the farm to me."

"How is that the right thing? My uncle left me the farm. I've developed a business that's going to start bringing in money tomorrow. I like living in Peculiar." She nodded to the tray on the table. "Coffee?"

He sat down and poured himself a cup. "Women can't run a farm. You can't trust Steve to come and do all the work. Now that he's got a baby, he's going to want a better job. Then where will you be? Out here, alone at night? I'm sure Martin's going to want his dog back sooner or later."

"I'll hire someone else. I'll get my own dog. I'm just as capable of running a farm as any man. Besides, that's not why you want the farm, is it?" She set her cup down and stared at him. "You aren't looking for a place to retire."

He didn't look at her. "I'm not sure what you mean."

"The highway that they're proposing runs right through the farm. You'd not only get the money from the state for the easements, but you'd also be able to sell the rest of the land for commercial development. Maybe a bigger grocery or hardware store? Maybe a car dealership?"

"Actually, I do have some connections with an automotive dealer who wants to build here for all these country folk who don't want to drive into Kansas City. I'm sure there will be other businesses too. Clever girl." He set his cup down. "How did you find out about the highway?"

"I went to the county courthouse to look at the farm plat." Rhoda wouldn't tell him why she'd wanted to look at the papers. She didn't want to throw Mr. Oaks under the bus. "Those women in the office were chatty about the new development."

"Women. They're always behind the gossip, aren't they?" He stood and paced the porch.

"Don't blame them. I found out tonight that you were the one who bought the canning salt when I talked with Arnold Ness. I thought you said your wife didn't can." She saw the shocked look on his face.

"I could have been buying it for someone else to use." He shook his head. "You don't have anything on me."

"Maybe not yet. But I talked with someone at the festival who saw your car out here that night and the night my ditch got damaged. I think with that testimony and the salt, the sheriff may at least take me seriously when I call him tomorrow and tell him what you've been doing. At the very least, when people hear what I have to say, that should keep you from actually forcing me to sell."

"Who do you think they'll believe? Someone who showed up last month, or their mayor? So what's it going to be? Do I have to keep ruining your land before you wake up and sell me the farm? I don't care if I have to salt every last inch of the place. Or maybe I'll just drown your plants in weed killer or motor oil? The people who want to build here won't worry about what can grow on the land. They're going to cover it with pavement anyway."

"So let me see if I understand my options. Either I sell to you, or you're going to continue vandalizing my property? Like you did with the sign and the irrigation ditch? And how you tried to salt my field, but Bo scared you away the other night?" Rhoda watched as he slowly grinned at her.

"I'm only trying to convince you to see logic. It's not personal. I tried to buy the farm as soon as I found out about the highway, but your uncle didn't want to move. Then he died before I could convince him." He pulled paper and a pen out of his pocket.

She let out a gasp, covering her mouth. "Did you hurt him?"

"Oh, don't be so dramatic. I didn't kill Fred. He had a heart attack." He held up his hand in a three-finger salute. "Scout's honor. Anyway, sign here, and I'll get you a check first thing Monday when the banks open. Then you can pack up your clothes and ugly shoes and go back to the city where you won't stick out like a sore thumb."

She took the paper and the pen. Then she set it down on the table and refilled her coffee cup. When that was done, she stood and took a step toward the door. "Is that enough?"

"Is what enough?" Terrance looked at her. He pointed to the paper. "That's all I'm paying you for this land. Just sign the contract."

"I think she was talking to me." Sheriff John Collins stepped out of the house and stood between Terrance and Rhoda. "Mayor Powers, you're under arrest for vandalism and whatever other charges the district attorney tells me I can charge you with. Maybe conspiracy, but I'm sure we'll figure it out."

Rhoda felt Martin come to stand next to her. His arm circled her waist, and Bo stood in front of her, softly growling as they watched the sheriff put handcuffs on the mayor. As another officer led the mayor away to the barn where their squad cars were hidden, the sheriff turned back to her.

"I'm so sorry your welcome to Peculiar was a little rocky. I sure hope this doesn't taint your enthusiasm for staying around. I'll be in touch if you need to testify at our good mayor's hearing." He stepped off the porch. "Bobby, grab the mayor's keys so we can impound his car and get it out of Miss Grey's driveway."

"I can ask my mom to come over and stay tonight if you want." Martin took Rhoda's coffee cup away and replaced it with a glass of milk. He was worried the sting had been too hard on her. She was still shaking even though they'd moved into the house and he had wrapped her in a blanket. He'd been right there with the sheriff if Powers had tried something, but it must have been scary. "I'm afraid to leave you alone."

"I wanted to go stargazing tonight. The moon's bright light is calling me. Maybe I should become an astronaut. Although I think my height might preclude me from being accepted into the program." Rhoda laughed and pulled the lap blanket tighter around her shoulders. Bo warmed her feet. "Instead, I'm making myself some hot cocoa and then heading upstairs to get some sleep. I can't believe this is over. I can't believe it was about money."

"Actually, the possibility of money. Sheriff Collins told me that the county has two different sites picked out and the other one is higher on the list. Mayor Powers might have just been left with a farm to try to run." Martin studied Rhoda's movements. She seemed solid, despite the shaking, but he was still concerned. "And you'd make an excellent astronaut."

"I'm not sure that's true." She was craving the cocoa. "And that would have been good for you. You might have been able to get the farm cheap when he realized he wasn't getting his big payout."

"I can think of other ways to expand my farm." He smiled as he took a pan from the cupboard. Yes, there was a way to expand Oaks Farm, but he thought they needed some time before he brought it up. "So, walk me through this hot cocoa thing. You've got people showing up to pick strawberries in less than nine hours."

"Are you having a cup too?" She met his gaze, and for a second, neither one said anything. When he nodded, she listed off the ingredients. Milk, sugar, cocoa, and salt. Then she walked him through the process to make cocoa for two.

He stirred the mixture as he watched her stroke Bo's head. "I'm sorry we had to do that. But we didn't have enough evidence with just his salt-buying habits."

"It was fine. I didn't want to keep playing this game. Getting him to admit to the vandalism at least gave the sheriff a reason to hold him. I think Peculiar is going to be having a special election soon." She tilted her head. "Maybe your dad should think about running. It would give him something to do."

"I'll bring it up Sunday. Are you coming for dinner?" He took the pan off the heat and took out two cups.

She didn't answer until he brought the cups to the table and sat down next to her. "Am I invited?"

"As long as I can take you out for ice cream later." He nodded to the cocoa. "If you've stopped shaking by then."

Chapter Ten

The next morning, between the birds singing and the sunshine in her eyes, Rhoda woke to the blessing of a new day. She lay in bed for a few minutes just listening. This was her new life. She now lived in the country, where she could work the land, grow her plants, and even talk to them without people thinking she was weird. No more getting up while it was still dark to get on a bus. No more sitting alone where no one talked to her on her ride to work. No more spending all day in an artificially lit cubicle, moving files from one pile to another. Eating lunch alone, riding back to her apartment on a bus, and then repeating the cycle, day after day.

In Baltimore, she didn't have friends. She didn't even have a pet unless you counted her plants.

Now, she had acres of strawberries, fields that needed to be planted, watered, and taken care of. She had friends, like Steve, Savannah, and Chet. And of course, Martin.

Martin. What were they? Friends? Now that they were done with their joint investigation, would he be just a neighbor? Someone who waved when he drove by, but not much more?

He'd invited her to dinner with his folks tomorrow. *And ice cream*, she reminded herself. Was that his code to let her know he wanted to date her?

She got up and started getting ready. She could worry about all the things she didn't know about dating and men while she was being productive. Last night at the festival, people had said they were coming today.

Her heart squeezed. What if they were just being nice? What if no one showed up for the grand opening? What if she couldn't sell enough to make the farm profitable? Martin had said he'd buy it, so maybe that would happen. And maybe that was what he'd meant about other ways to expand Oaks Farm.

Rhoda finished her braid and went downstairs to make herself some oatmeal. She might be too nervous to eat, but at least this way she'd have something to do besides worry while she waited. Why had she even thought she could do this?

She washed the dishes from the night before while her oatmeal cooked. Then she forced herself to eat while watching the clock. At seven forty-five, she washed the last dirty spoon and let the water out of the sink. After drying her hands on a towel, she folded it then went into the living room. There she picked up the cashbox she'd bought and filled a few days ago and then pulled on her sweater. She took a jug of tea out of the fridge and put it in the large canvas tote with the other items and two plastic cups. One for her, one for Steve.

She left the house and walked down the driveway to the roadside stand. Steve was already there and had parked in the gravel area they'd made for customers. He opened the shutters that covered the window at night. The shutters doubled as an awning for people standing outside the shed.

"Hey boss, ready for a busy day?" He grinned as he set up the final pole on the last shutter. "What do you think of the shed?"

"You did a great job. This is amazing." She went inside, arranged her small cash table, and put the bag with the tea and cups under it. Then she went outside and lined up the small baskets of strawberries Steve had picked yesterday. Steve hung a sign on the shed by her cash window and then stacked picking buckets near the side.

When they were done, they stood there and studied the white and red shed. "It looks happy."

"I think it looks lucky." Steve adjusted a stack of buckets. "Your U-pick strawberry field is going to be amazing."

She looked over at the almost empty parking lot. Steve's old truck sat there, alone. "Now all we need are customers."

He looked at his watch. "They'll come. It's not quite eight."

"I don't know. I wonder if this was a bad idea." Rhoda sank down at the picnic table Steve had moved next to the shed. A place for families to eat lunch or rest before or after doing their strawberry picking. "I mean, no one else does this type of sales process here. I should have focused on stores. Arnold Ness wants me to come by on Monday with some stock. I could make jam and sell that to the stores as well. I want to keep the farm. Now that the threat of having to sell it is over, I'm scared that it isn't going to be profitable enough to keep everything running."

"Your uncle ran this farm for years. It's profitable. And that was without your new U-pick plan to bring in more revenue. If this doesn't work, we'll go back to Fred's plan. But it's going to work. Believe me. If I didn't think you were going to be able to afford me, I would have gone to work with Oaks Farm after Fred died. I've got a family to support, and I'm putting my faith in you and James Farm."

She wiped the lone tear that had fallen while Steve talked. She wasn't alone. If this plan didn't work, they'd go on to Plan B or Plan C or whatever they needed to do. She wasn't going to give up. Steve and his family counted on the farm being successful. Somehow that made Rhoda feel better. Hopeful.

And as if Steve had opened the floodgates with his optimism, a car, then two, then five headed down the road toward them and parked in the lot. Steve grinned at her. "I told you people were going to come."

Rhoda watched as families piled out of cars. Some had brought their own buckets, some had brought their children, and all had brought big smiles. The good folk of Peculiar had come out to support her. One of their own.

She lifted up a quick prayer of thanks and hurried into the shed. It was time to start her new life.

Martin pulled into Rhoda's driveway just after the U-pick shed closed for the night. He saw her sitting on the porch, counting the day's take. He'd been busy at the farm most of the day and hadn't had time to get away to congratulate her before now. Being a farmer was hard work, even with help from his employees. He could have continued working long into the night, but he'd learned one thing from his father. He needed to create a balance between living on the farm and working the farm. He had to have boundaries.

When the workday ended, a farmer didn't bring work home from the barn unless it was an emergency. There were enough of those in the worst of times. He didn't have to make everything urgent.

He opened the truck door and reached for the bouquet of roses he'd picked when he'd gone home to shower off the day's dust and sweat. Bo had decided to come with him, so the dog jumped over the roses and ran up to greet Rhoda. Martin smiled at Bo's exuberance. He felt the same way, but he played it cool. Bo had no shame. He loved Rhoda and didn't worry about showing it.

Maybe there were lessons he could learn from his dog as well. He met her gaze and smiled. "You had a great day, at least from the number of cars I saw coming up and down our road."

She closed the cashbox and set it on the table. Then she tapped it. "The money seems to corroborate your observation. Hopefully, it wasn't a sign of just supporting a local business on opening day. Sorry, scratch that. Steve told me I'm supposed to be more optimistic."

"Steve is a pretty levelheaded guy. If he says you should look at the day as a positive sign, I'd believe him." He came up the stairs, keeping the roses behind his back.

"Actually, it was an amazing day. I had several people ask when I was going to be open again. I've officially set my days for Wednesday and Saturday for the next couple of weeks. Steve's making us a new sign to replace the paper one I put up about noon, since I had gotten so many questions about that." Rhoda rolled her shoulders.

"That's great." He handed her the bouquet. "These are to celebrate your new business. May your success bloom as brightly as these roses."

"You know, red roses aren't a symbol of new beginnings. That's yellow or white roses. But I appreciate the thought." She took the roses and stood. "I'll go put these in a vase. They'll look lovely in the foyer."

"Rhoda, I know what red roses mean." He stepped closer, blocking her way into the house. "I was hoping my intentions would be implied."

She froze by her chair. "What intentions?"

He laughed and took a breath. "You're not making this easy."

She shrugged, searching his face for a clue. "I'm sorry, but I don't know what you're saying."

He came closer and took her hand in his. "I'm saying that I want to date you, Miss Grey. Let's see where this attraction leads. I can't get you out of my head."

She laughed, and he dropped her hand.

"I guess I misread the signs?" He stepped back. "I hope this brief moment of insanity doesn't affect our friendship."

She grabbed his hand and pulled him closer. "No, you didn't misread the signs. Sorry, I laugh when I'm nervous. I would love to figure out where this attraction is going as well."

"Then that's settled." He let out a long breath, picked up her cashbox, and opened the door. "I know we have dinner plans tomorrow, but can I take you to supper tonight? There's a lovely restaurant on the way to Kansas City. Not too far away but still a nice drive. We can eat out on the patio, and they don't mind if we bring Bo."

"That sounds delightful. I would hate to have to leave Bo in the house all by himself again. We did a lot of that this week." She rubbed Bo's head as the three of them went inside. "Just give me a few minutes to freshen up."

"I'll take care of these." He reached for the roses, and she headed upstairs. He put the cashbox on the dining room table and went to the kitchen to put the roses in water. When that was done, he took them out to the foyer and put them on the table by the door. Rhoda had been right. The flowers added something to the room. His gaze wandered back to the dining room table.

in Peculiar, Missouri

The plat of the farm was still on the table, and she'd drawn with crayons on the white paper. Strawberries in the front and back field that bordered his property. Then there was a band of green with gold flowers drawn inside the green border. Underneath the band she'd written the word *marigolds*.

She was using plants to keep bugs away. He wondered about his own plans to spray the young corn sprouts with chemicals. Maybe there was another way. He looked up and saw her standing in the doorway in a blue dress and matching flats, watching him. "What do you think?"

"From what I've seen, you've got a great plan." He stood and walked over to her. "I've got a lot of questions about natural farming, but that can wait. Right now, I just want to tell you how beautiful you look."

Chapter Eleven

As the summer wound down, Rhoda had more time to read the books Martin had loaned her. Her plans on how she was going to set up next summer's U-pick sales, roadside stands, and produce to sell to local grocery stores were coming together. The farm kept her busy, and she was always trying something new. Today marked the four-month anniversary of her move to Peculiar, and as she moved a pile of books off her desk, an envelope fell to the floor. She picked it up and realized it was the letter from her uncle. The one that Jacob Stine had given her months ago. The one she'd never read.

She went outside on the porch, and Bella, her black lab puppy, followed her. Bella never let Rhoda out of her sight. Unless she was napping. Which she did a lot. Growing puppies needed a lot of sleep, apparently. Martin had shown up one Friday afternoon soon after the successful grand opening of the U-pick stand with Bella in a basket wearing a large red bow. Rhoda had fallen in love with the puppy immediately. And just a little more of her heart had gone out to Martin Oaks.

She sat down, and Bella put her front paws on Rhoda's capris, asking to be lifted up onto her lap. Laughing, she picked her up and gave her a kiss on the head. She still had that wonderful puppy smell. "Pretty soon you're going to be too big to do this, so enjoy it while you can."

in Peculiar, Missouri

Bella licked Rhoda's arm in response and then curled up into a ball to sleep. Rhoda ran a hand down her soft fur and opened the letter.

Dear Rhododendron,

I know you hate that name, but your mother and I were raised by people who treasured the land and the plants that grow on the earth. Your grandparents were farmers as were those who came before them. Rhoda, your full name is full of possibilities. It's a name that makes people smile around you and one that is a promise of your true beauty. Your mother told me that you were teased at school because you inherited the James family height. We're all tall around here. It's not a curse. Now that you're older and away from those mean kids, I hope you realize how special you are. Your aunt Bea and I weren't blessed with children. A large family, which we both wanted, wasn't in the cards for us. With her gone the last five years and your mother gone as well, you are my only family.

Now don't get me wrong. I have friends and family of my heart here in Peculiar, Missouri. It's been a wonderful place to live my life. And so, I wanted to leave you James Farm so that you could experience the love I've felt from the caring people of Peculiar. They don't judge. They help when they're needed. All in all, it's a great place to live. So please, don't sell the farm. Not until you've lived here for a while.

Of course, it's up to you. I'm just an old man who doesn't have much time left here on Earth, or any right to direct your path. But if you're looking for family when you get this after my death, Peculiar will fill that need. You just have to be open to hearing its siren call.

Remember, you were always loved.

Uncle Frederick James

She set the letter on the table and let his words sink in. He'd known she must have been lonely all on her own in Baltimore, so he'd given her a home. Finding family and friends to fill up other parts of her life had been up to her.

Bella jumped off her lap and went out to the yard to run around. Rhoda started to follow her and then sank down on the steps. The day was hot, and she closed her eyes and lifted her face to take in the sun's rays. She felt her family's love. Just sitting here on the family farm. She was home.

She heard the sound of a truck pulling off the road and onto the driveway. Rhoda hurried to pick up Bella before she decided to run out in the driveway to meet the visitor. She swooped the dog up into her arms just as Martin's truck came into view. She waited for him to park then walked over to greet him and Bo. Martin pulled her into an embrace and kissed her gently.

"So what's up today?" he asked as he let her go and took Bella into his arms.

Rhoda pointed to the porch. "I finally read the letter Uncle Fred left me."

"Fred left you a letter?" Martin had been friends with her uncle before he died. A fact that she was thankful for. At least he wasn't alone after his wife passed on.

in Peculiar, Missouri

"He did." She handed him the letter and took Bella. Bo sat next to her chair, begging for some attention. She scratched behind his ears while Martin read the letter and Bella mauled her newest chew toy.

He finished and grinned up at her. "So, Rhododendron, huh?"

"You read that lovely letter about how wonderful Peculiar and its people are, and that's all you can do? Tease me about my name?" She snapped her fingers at Bo and pointed to his master. "Go bite him."

"I was kidding. But it is a fun fact. Your uncle was one of Peculiar's biggest fans. He always supported the festivals, and he paid for the Christmas lights one year when the town didn't have the money to put them up." He put the letter back in the envelope. "You're a lot like him."

"Why do you say that?" How could she be like an uncle she didn't know and had only met a few times?

"You're strong. You don't give up when you know what you want. And you're always helping the underdog." Martin put the letter on the table.

"That's me, Saint Rhoda." She kissed Bo's head. "Following in her uncle's footsteps."

"Don't believe me then. I just came over to make sure we're still on for tonight. Mom said she'll watch Bella and Bo, so we're free to actually go to dinner." He laughed and stood. Then he looked down at the diamond he'd put on her hand last weekend. "Oh, and be prepared. Mom wants to talk about when we're doing the engagement party. She wants to have it at the house or in the church basement. It depends on who we're asking to celebrate with us."

Rhoda turned the ring on her finger. "We can talk about that. I don't have any out-of-town family or friends to invite, so I guess your list is longer."

"You might not have family outside of Peculiar, but you've made a lot of friends since you've moved here. You should think about who you want to invite as well." He pulled her to her feet and into his arms. "You're a force of nature, Rhoda Grey. Everyone you meet is affected by your spirit. Don't forget it."

"I'll think about a list. I'll be ready at five. Today's kind of a bum-around day. I wasn't quite sure what I wanted to get done, then Bella and the letter distracted me." She knew she needed to invite Steve and his wife. And Arnold Ness, who'd become a friend as well as a vendor for her produce. And then the women from Savannah's book club. Maybe she did have more than a few people she wanted at the party. She picked up the envelope and pressed it to her chest as she strolled to the door. "I guess I'll go clean house for a few hours before we go out. I don't want the day to just disappear on me."

"Days can do that. Especially if you have a good book and want to spend the afternoon reading." He slapped his leg, and Bo came running. Bella followed Rhoda.

"Don't tempt me. I need to figure out my next great idea and get the house cleaned. Maybe vacuuming will help me think about my list in a more productive manner." She leaned on the doorframe. "Thank you for welcoming me to Peculiar. I love my new life."

"You should thank the whole town. I was just trying to keep my farm safe from being attacked by random vandals like yours." He smiled as he leaned on the porch column.

in Peculiar, Missouri

"How, exactly, do I thank the entire town?" she asked.

He returned to the truck to get something and then came back to the porch with a newspaper. He handed it to her. "I've been thinking about this. Here's this week's *Peculiar Times*. Maybe you should write a letter to the editor?"

She glanced at the headline. The front page was filled with national news, mostly about the upcoming election. Kennedy versus Nixon. Even in newsprint, Mr. Kennedy looked nicer. But when she opened the paper, she saw letters to the local editor about all kinds of things. Martin was right. A letter in the paper would at least reach those people who subscribed.

She kissed Martin goodbye, tucked the paper under her arm, and went inside. Back to the dining room table she'd turned into her desk. She considered the mess and thought she should move all this stuff to her actual office and work there. Then she could invite people over for dinner. But Martin's words continued to echo in her head. Maybe she *should* thank the whole town.

She picked up a pen and twisted it in her hand. A letter to the editor. It wasn't a bad idea. What should she say? She thought for a few moments and then started writing.

> *Dear town of Peculiar,*
> *When I came here, I was alone. I had no family left, no friends. All I had in life was my work and my plants. My work wasn't fulfilling, and when my plants were destroyed on the rooftop of my Baltimore apartment, I decided I needed to do something else, to be somewhere else. So I moved here to*

the farm my uncle left me in his will. That one decision changed my life, and I'm so grateful.

She couldn't wait to see what happened to her and the farm next. She set the pen down and picked up Bella. Home wasn't just where you slept, it was where you lived. And now, she was living.

Love Fits

by
Laura Bradford

A single act of kindness throws out roots in all directions, and the roots spring up and make new trees.

—Amelia Earhart

Chapter One

Peculiar, Missouri
Present Day

Susie Walker straightened the hem of her white eyelet blouse, drew in a deep breath, and knocked on the partially opened door marked Office. "Excuse me, Mr. Bonner?"

The telltale sound of a chair's leg scraping against a floorboard was followed seconds later by a clipped invitation to enter delivered by way of a deep, almost rumbly voice. Squaring her shoulders, Susie pushed the door open the rest of the way to find a dark-haired young man seated behind a simple metal desk, his attention moving between an opened notebook to his right and a printed list of some sort on his left. "Mr. Brian Bonner?" she repeated. "I'm Susie Walker. I spoke with you on the phone the other day about renting a booth here. I have the paperwork you requested and a check for my first month's rent."

Setting his pen atop the notebook page, he glanced up, gave her the same double take she'd been getting since she was old enough to dress herself, and slowly leaned back in his chair, his amusement evident in the twinkle of his chocolate-brown eyes. "Wow. I—I don't know what to say."

"Trust me, few people do." She closed the gap between the doorway and the desk with one long step, set her paperwork and check on top of his notebook, and met his lingering disbelief with her usual smile. "But no worries. All I need is for you to tell me everything is good with the forms and point me in the direction of my booth."

His gaze traveled from the tips of her bow-tied braids to her sunshine-yellow polka-dot skirt and her equally sunshine-yellow rain boots and back up again. "You're very...cheerful."

"Thank you."

She watched as he forced his attention first onto her check and then, finally, her paperwork. "You're calling your booth Square Peg Susie's?" he asked, looking at her again.

She spread her arms and did a little turn where she stood. "Can you think of a better name?"

"So that's"—he gestured to Susie's attire—"just a gimmick, then?"

"You mean this?" She looked down at her clothes. "Nope. No gimmick. This is me as I am and the way I've always been."

"I see."

"Needless to say, I didn't have to look too far for booth-naming inspiration."

Again, he looked at the paperwork, his eyes darting back and forth as he read his way to the bottom. "You're from Connecticut?" he asked, glancing up once again.

"Until about a week ago, yes."

"And now?"

"I'm living above Peculiar Books on Main Street."

He drew back, surprised. "I know where it is, but... Marge is renting that second-floor space out? To be lived in?"

Susie nodded.

"It is even habitable?" he asked.

"In the most basic of ways, yes," Susie said, shrugging. "But that's what an imagination is for, yes?"

He stared at her for a moment and then took a quick glance back at her paperwork. "How'd you find your way to Peculiar, Missouri, of all places?"

Her answering laugh echoed its way around the windowless room. "Don't you think the better question is what took someone like *me*"—again, she spread her arms—"so long to find it?"

"You said it, not me." He grinned.

"I know I did." She pointed at the paperwork and the check and then hooked her thumb toward the door at her back. "So? Am I cleared for a booth? I'd really like to get in here and start setting up so I can be up and running by the time Saturday morning rolls around."

Again, Brian consulted the forms. "You're selling candles? And wind chimes? And jams? And cupcakes? And…" He pulled the paper closer. "An old typewriter?"

"Yes to all, except the typewriter. That's just something I'll have out on a table for people wanting to share a thought, an observation, a favorite poem or verse, or whatever strikes their fancy in the moment."

He looked up, frowning. "For what it's worth, I'm finding that the most successful booths we have here seem to be ones that are very specific in their offerings. Meaning, they pick one—maybe two—things and focus on that."

She felt her shoulders start to slump and willed them back into place. "But I don't have to, right? I mean, as long as I'm not selling anything illegal, I can choose my own inventory, right?"

"Absolutely. Of course. But—"

"I appreciate your concern and your expertise, I really do. But I've got a vision in my head, and I'd like to see it through. My way."

"The Square Peg Susie way?" he quipped.

She grinned. "Yes, the Square Peg Susie way."

He took one last look at her paperwork, relocated it to a wire basket behind his desk, and then pushed back his chair. "Okay. Let me show you your booth, and you can start setting up any time after five o'clock tonight."

She didn't mean to squeal, but she couldn't stop herself. "I am so, so excited!"

His laugh wasn't unkind. "I can see that." He started to come out from around his desk but stopped before he'd cleared the corner. "Actually, since you're so excited, would you mind giving Art Cummings at *The Peculiar Times* a call? He's putting together a feature story about Bonner's Open-Air Market for this week's paper. You know, stuff like what made me start it, how it's going, what my plans are for it in the future, et cetera."

"Sounds like wonderful PR for you," she mused.

"It is. But it could be for you as well."

"Me?"

Brian reached down, pulled a blank page from his notebook, and quickly scrawled the reporter's name and number on it before holding it out for Susie. "I know Art has already talked to a few of my vendors, but I'm sure he'd be happy to talk to you too, seeing as how you're new to Peculiar and all."

"Right. Sure. Of course." She took the paper and stuffed it inside the striped canvas shoulder tote that doubled as her purse. "Thank you. I'll reach out to him this afternoon."

"Perfect." Motioning for her to follow, Brian led the way out the door and into the covered pavilion space that made up Bonner's Open-Air Market. "Now, let's go see where Square Peg Susie's will be come Saturday morning, shall we?"

Chapter Two

More than a few times, Susie wanted to stop and pinch herself to make sure she wasn't dreaming, but since the moment her sunflower watch had hit nine o'clock, she'd been on the move answering questions, making suggestions, and ringing up countless purchases.

In the lead-up to Square Peg Susie's first day, she'd planned to keep record of her sales in the glittery yellow and blue notebook she'd bought at a gift shop on her trek from Connecticut to Missouri. But as busy as she'd been since her first customer had approached, even her intended tally mark system proved too much.

It was a good problem to have, she knew. As was the growing need to restock just about every shelf in her booth before the next market day rolled around.

Glancing around at her space, she noted the dwindling candle supply, the empty cupcake case, and the last jar of blueberry jam before landing her attention and her smile on the basket of hair bows much like the ones tied around her own ponytails.

"Looks like your first day has been a smashing success so far."

The familiar voice lassoed her attention back to the counter and the pair of eyes that called to mind any number of delectable chocolate treats. "Mr. Bonner. Hello."

"You say Mr. Bonner, and I look for my dad. So, to keep me from whipping my head around unnecessarily, let's just go with Brian."

"Brian," she repeated, only to hold up her finger as a young girl she guessed to be about ten plunked a pair of lilac-colored hair bows on the counter. Shifting her focus to the paying customer, Susie bagged up the bows and swapped them for the five-dollar bill held out in her direction. "These will look darling on you, sweetheart."

The girl's face flushed pink before she disappeared into the crowd meandering up and down the pavilion's center aisle. When she was out of sight, Susie turned back to Brian. "I don't know how I can ever properly thank you for pointing me toward that reporter. It seems just about everyone who has stopped by so far today read that article."

"I'm sure they did," he said, rocking back on the heels of his work boots. "Your story was rather endearing."

"Your friend asked good questions."

"I'm pretty sure he asked everyone the same ones." He took in her sunflower-adorned summer romper, the dark green bows around her ponytails, and her simple white Keds, and then lifted his gaze to hers. "What? No rain boots today?"

"Not today."

His attention lingered on her for a few beats more before he moved to the small table just inside the opening of her booth. "So that's the typewriter you talked about in the article? The one your customers can type messages on?"

"It is."

"I think that's a pretty cool idea."

"Thank you."

"Any takers yet?" Brian asked.

"Other than the one that was waiting for me when I got here, I don't know. I've been too busy to check since I loaded in a new piece of paper." Crossing to the table, she turned the typewriter's roller knob to reveal a half dozen or so *hellos*, one *this is cool*, one line showcasing every letter in the alphabet, and one of her favorite Bible verses of all time. "Oh. Joshua 1:9. I love that verse, don't you?"

Brian, stepped beside her, his brow furrowed. "I do, actually. But you said there was a message waiting when you got here?"

"That's right. See?" She grabbed hold of the paper she'd set aside and handed it to Brian.

"'I am a square peg too,'" he read aloud.

"Yes. And they also left me this." She held up the handcrafted pencil box she'd found beside the typewriter and turned it slowly so as to show off the skill that clearly went into making it. "Isn't it gorgeous?"

He looked from the pencil box to the typed note and, finally, back to Susie. "What time did you get here?"

"I got here at six thirty this morning. Early, I know, but I wanted to make sure everything was the way I wanted it before the doors opened at nine."

"And was anyone else here at that time?" he asked. "Vendor-wise?"

She shook her head. "Just me. For probably the first hour or so, I guess."

"No one, other than the vendors, are supposed to be in here before—or after—hours."

"Nothing was missing, if that's what you're worried about," she said, shrugging. "There was just this one sentence typed on the paper I'd loaded into the typewriter when I left last night, and the pencil box. That's it."

in Peculiar, Missouri

He rubbed his chin in frustration. "I'm sorry about this, Susie. I'll talk to the police chief and make sure his crew is running some patrols out here."

"Please don't," she said, gently gripping his arm. "I don't think the person who typed *this*"—she pointed from the sheet of paper to the pencil box—"and left *that* meant any harm. I...I think they were just reaching out. That's all."

"They were trespassing, Susie."

She frowned. "They didn't do any harm."

"*This* time, maybe," Brian conceded, shrugging. "But still, this is private property. I don't need to be worrying that your stuff—or any of the other vendors' stuff—is going to get ripped off."

"I'm not worried," she said. "Truly, I'm—"

"Excuse me, miss? Can I ask you a question?"

She looked past Brian to a woman standing just inside the entrance of the booth with a mesmerized expression on her tanned face. "I'm sorry. I really have to get back to work."

"No apologies." Brian shot another look in the direction of the mysterious note before mustering a parting smile for Susie. "Congratulations again on what's clearly been a very successful first day."

"Thanks, Brian."

He took a step. Stopped. Looked back, his smile at the ready once again. "For what it's worth, I predict those hair bows of yours are going to be selling like hotcakes before long."

"Oh?" she asked. "Why's that?"

"Because you're a great model for them."

And then, just like that, he was gone, her warm cheeks and the waiting customer's knowing smile all the proof she needed that she had, in fact, heard him correctly.

For the first time all day, it was quiet. No questions being asked. No kids laughing or crying in the distance. No cell phones ringing. No crinkle of bags. No jingle of change. No swiping of the credit card machine. And—she scanned the booths to her left and right—no sign of any of her fellow vendors.

It had been a good first day. An amazing first day, actually. The kind of day she'd always hoped for but had been reticent to actually believe would happen.

"Not too bad for a square peg," she said aloud, the echo of her words giving new oomph to her tired smile and aching muscles.

If she had a cell phone, she'd take a picture of Square Peg Susie's empty shelves—maybe even make it a selfie. But since she didn't, she'd have to settle for committing the sight, and the feeling it invoked, to memory so she could pull it out and dust if off anytime she needed proof that there wasn't anything wrong with her ideas and her dreams. They, like her, were just different. And different didn't have to be wrong.

Stretching her arms above her head, she allowed herself a quick yawn before packing up her tote bag and notebook and heading for home.

Home…

For the first time in her life, home could be however she wanted it to be. She didn't have to be teased about her decorations, eyed with amusement when she walked out of her room in whatever outfit she'd assembled for the day, or hear how strange she was all the time. No, here, in Peculiar, Missouri, behind the walls of her little apartment over the bookstore, she could feel good about being herself.

She didn't need a mirror or a camera to know she was smiling. She could feel it deep inside her soul. And oh, how wonderful it felt.

Slowly at first, and then with gathering speed born of pure joy, Susie turned round and round on the tips of her Keds, her arms outstretched. People liked her candles! People liked her cupcakes! People liked her jams! People liked her bracelets! People liked—

She stopped suddenly as her gaze fell on the oft-asked-about pencil box she could've sold ten times over that day if only she knew who'd left it and whether it was, in fact, okay to sell. Crossing to the box, Susie fingered the finely sanded wood, the beveled edges, and the flower petals etched into the front panel.

Who made it?

Why did they leave it for her?

Slanting her gaze back to the sheet of paper she'd pulled from the machine that morning, she eyed the six words in the center.

I AM A SQUARE PEG TOO.

Six words that could just be the work of someone being silly. Maybe a gaggle of bored teenagers looking for fun on a Friday night? Maybe a member of the market's maintenance crew who'd had a moment of boredom? Maybe...

No.

Whoever had typed those words meant them. She'd bet every penny she'd made today on that fact.

Her mind made up, she pulled out the sheet of paper customers had been typing on throughout the day and replaced it with the one she'd removed upon her arrival that morning. Then, turning the knob, she brought herself to the empty white space below those six words and lined her fingers up on the keys.

YOUR WORK IS LOVELY.
YOU SHOULD SELL THE THINGS YOU MAKE.

When she reached the end of her second line, she stopped and considered what else she could write, but, in the end, she left it alone. Time would tell if her fellow square peg would see it and respond before the market reopened on Tuesday morning. If he or she did, they'd go from there. In the meantime, though, she was starving.

Susie grabbed her notebook, shoved it into her tote bag, and made her way past her colleagues' empty booths and out into the fresh, early evening air. She drew in a deep breath, savored the hint of lilacs she detected, and readied herself for a most satisfied exhale when she was cut short by the sound of voices. Mocking. Teasing.

"Hey, Big Ears!"

She turned toward the sound.

"Looks like your head has doors that are wiiiiiide open!"

Making haste in the direction of the laughter that followed, she came around the line of hedges between Bonner's Open-Air Market and the small park on the southern end of Main Street. She spotted two teenage boys—one redhead, the other a brunette—pointing and yelling at a third boy, roughly their same age, who was walking a clearly old dog on a leash.

"Do those things make a wind noise when you walk, buddy boy?" the redhead fairly cackled.

"Be careful, your brains might fall out if you take that corner too fast, Big Ears!" said the brunette.

"Hey!" Susie clapped her hands, once. Hard. "Stop that right now!"

Startled, the redhead turned, in unison with his friend, toward Susie. "Who? Us?" the brunette asked, his voice dripping with incredulity.

Out of the corner of her eye, she saw the young dog walker stop, look over his shoulder in their direction, and then go into the woods, glancing back every few feet as Susie focused her full attention on the bullies. "Yes. You."

"Why? Did you see his ears?"

She held the teen's glare. "No, but I see yours…"

"His are *huge*."

"And?" she countered, her voice calm, steady. "So what?"

"C'mon, Liam," said the redhead, tugging on his friend's arm. "Let's go."

Liam paused for a moment as if he might say something else, but, in the end, he just pinned Susie with another, harder glare before falling in step behind his friend. A few feet from the road, though, he looked back, the ugliness of his previous words still evident on his face.

"Next time, why don't you just mind your own business," he spat.

"Be kind, and I will."

Chapter Three

Susie opened the window above the kitchen sink and breathed in the potpourri of aromas that collided inside her tiny apartment above Peculiar Books. There was the fragrant smell of lilacs from the hedge opposite her window, the hearty scent of dark-roasted coffee beans pumping out of the Beanery Café to her right, the vanilla, lavender, and amber base notes still lingering from Saturday night's candle-making session, and the stomach-teasing whiff of some sort of appley goodness from the breakfast place to her left.

Smiling, she stepped back, returned her freshly washed breakfast plate to its rightful spot inside the second of only three cabinets, and made her way into her new living room. A couch, if she had one, would take up more than half the space all on its own, but she didn't mind. This room and this apartment were hers. Hers to decorate, hers to make memories in, hers to be herself in without feeling different.

If she wanted to paint the whole apartment in the same shade of yellow, she could.

If she wanted to make a half-dozen angel figures and hang them from a mobile, she could.

If she wanted to dance her way from room to room for no particular reason, she could.

And she would. If she wanted to.

Today, though, her focus was on this room. The soft sunshine hue of the walls she'd painted during the wee hours of the night helped offset the limited natural light, as she'd known it would. The medley of pale blue throw pillows she'd been sewing all week promised to add a nice pop of color to the cream-colored futon due to be delivered in—she checked her watch—roughly one hour. And the vintage stepladder she'd spotted between customers at the market on Saturday would make a fun way to finally display the kind of treasures that spoke to her rather than the magazine-worthy feel of her childhood home.

Here, she didn't have to worry whether the ballerina in her music box was missing a shoe.

Here, she could fill her bookshelves with her paperback cozy mysteries without worry of being judged over her "simplistic" reading choices.

And here, she didn't have to stash the pictures she painted in her closet in favor of the pricey artwork deemed more worthy of hanging on walls people might see.

In other words, she could be Square Peg Susie to her heart's content in this place because it—

"Is mine," Susie whispered. "All mine."

It was a refreshing feeling. Even heady, at times. And she loved every minute of it. Had she always dressed to please herself? Yes. Had she always hummed and danced her way from place to place like someone out of an old black-and-white movie? Yes. But at least here, some 1,300 miles away from where her family had always lived, she could be and do those things without having to worry about embarrassing her siblings at every turn.

Yes, she knew her brother and sister loved her. She'd never doubted that. But just as she'd always been the strange one at school for saving ants, making playthings from her classmates' discards, and befriending the other oddballs in the room, she'd also been the strange one at home. While her parents and siblings practically killed themselves working for expensive cars and large houses, Susie wanted to find another way—something more in keeping with one of the very first Bible passages she'd memorized on her own outside of Sunday School.

"Matthew 6:26," she whispered. "'Look at the birds of the air; they do not sow or reap or store away in barns, and yet your heavenly Father feeds them. Are you not much more valuable than they?'"

With God's grace and guidance, she'd finally gotten to a place where she knew the answer to Matthew's question. And now that she did, she wanted to live that way in a place where people either didn't see her as being odd all the time or didn't care that she was.

Shaking off her latest round of woolgathering, Susie secured a hammer and nail from her tool bag and the framed letter to the editor she'd been waiting to hang on her wall since the day she first stumbled across it. By placing it just inside the front door, she hoped it would serve as food for thought for the friends she hoped to make and entertain inside these four walls. It would also be a reminder to herself as to why she'd chosen this town as her forever home. And maybe, just maybe, she could one day share it with the mysterious person who clearly saw himself or herself as…different.

For a moment she allowed herself to imagine who might have left her the note on her typewriter and the handcrafted pencil box on the table beside it. More than a few times since Saturday, she'd revisited the note in her thoughts, the author's pain something she understood well. Too well, in fact.

Sighing, she turned back, held the nail in the desired spot, and hammered it into place. Then, swapping the hammer for the framed letter, she hung it, started to straighten it, and then, on second thought, opted to leave it a hairbreadth off center as a symbolic nod to the words she'd read at least a hundred times.

"'People saw past the things that had always made me different and opted to focus, instead, on my heart and soul,'" she murmured as her gaze fell on the same sentence that always seemed to leap out at her from the letter no matter how many times she held it, looked at it, studied it.

A loud grunt, followed by an even louder thump, drifted into the room, beckoning her back to the kitchen and the open window overlooking the alley. She looked to the right toward the Beanery—nothing. She looked left toward the bakery—nothing.

A second grunt, followed by another, more muted thump, tugged her focus forward, to the shared blue dumpster and the shock of white hair she could just make out around its far corner. A few feet away, atop an old rusty wagon, was what appeared to be an old window frame, a small wooden pallet that had seen better days, and a piece of broken shelving she knew had come from the bookstore the previous day.

Seconds later, after yet another scrap of wood she couldn't quite identify was plucked from the dumpster and tossed onto the wagon's pile, the scrap of white hair morphed into a man she guessed to be in his early eighties. Slowly, he hobbled over to the wagon, grabbed the long black handle, and—wheels squeaking—disappeared between a gap in the lilac-covered hedge line she hadn't noticed until that moment.

She rose up on her tiptoes in an attempt to make out any further sign of the man, but other than the hint of a fading whistle, there was nothing. Shrugging, she took one last whiff of the same scents from earlier and got back to the tasks at hand.

Chapter Four

She felt someone watching her as she stepped onto the sidewalk with the fourth and final box of inventory for the shelves of Square Peg Susie's and quickly scanned her surroundings. There was the pair of middle-aged women chatting over an early Tuesday morning coffee at one of the Beanery's outdoor tables… The young man getting in a run before his work day started… The delivery guy stacking boxes next to Peculiar Books' front door… And the pair of eyes that quickly disappeared behind a newspaper when Susie's gaze landed on the bench directly across from her apartment.

Hmm…

From her angle and without the benefit of being able to see an actual face behind the newspaper, Susie at least knew it was a woman. The bobby socks and crisp white sneakers that led to a flowered skirt told her that much. What they didn't tell her was why their glove-wearing owner didn't want to be caught watching Susie.

Shrugging, she stepped down off the sidewalk, slid the box into the last remaining empty spot in her car, and closed the door as, once again, she felt as if she was being watched. A glance at the bench just before she settled in behind the steering wheel yielded yet another hasty shuffle of the same newspaper on the same bench.

She readied her smile lest the woman look back one more time, but when the paper remained fully opened, she gave up in favor of the half-mile trek to the pavilion. A glance at her dashboard clock confirmed she had exactly an hour to get her new inventory unpacked and set up before Square Peg Susie's booth opened for its second day of business.

But unpack and set up she did, arranging her new scented candles alongside her flavored butters and jams and her cupcakes-of-the-day inside the clear case she'd purchased for them. By the time everything was set, she had ten minutes left to take a breath, ready her cash bag, and stage her notebook for the tally mark system she—

Pulling in a quick breath, Susie bypassed the tote bag on her chair in favor of the typewriter and the piece of paper that jutted out farther than it had when she left on Saturday evening.

Sure enough, just below the two sentences she'd typed were two more.

THANK YOU.
NO ONE WOULD BUY THINGS FROM ME.

"Why not?" she asked on the heels of a gasp. "That pencil box was absolutely—"

The rest of her words drifted away as a glance to the spot where the pencil box had been left on Saturday yielded the sweetest, most detailed birdhouse she'd ever seen. Stunned, she abandoned the typewriter in favor of the bird-sized Victorian home complete with gingerbread at the eaves, a two-story turret, a tiny front porch, and window-shaped holes for its intended occupants.

"Wow. Did you make that?"

Startled, Susie looked over her shoulder to find Brian looking from her to the birdhouse and back again, the wonder he wore surely a match of her own. "It's—it's incredible, isn't it?" she whispered. "I mean, the detail? The craftsmanship? It's...wow."

"So, I take it the answer to my question is no?"

"Question?" she echoed.

Brian ran his index finger along the birdhouse's miniature porch railing. "About whether you made this or not."

"No, I didn't make this."

"Are you selling it on consignment then?"

"No." She lowered the birdhouse to the table and motioned Brian over to the typewriter and the new message it contained. "My mystery visitor made it. See?"

Brian leaned forward, read the paper, and then pinned Susie with visible wariness. "This wasn't here when you closed up on Saturday?"

"No. I left this"—she rolled the paper down to make it easier for Brian to read the message she'd left in response to the first one—"just in case the person came by again. And, thankfully, they did."

"*Thankfully?*" Brian raked his hand through his hair. "You make it sound like this is a good thing. Like you *want* this person coming in here and messing around in your booth after hours."

She rolled the paper out of the typewriter and handed it to him while she loaded a clean sheet for her customers to use. "Whoever it is isn't doing any harm, Brian. They're just typing messages and leaving me beautiful handmade things."

"They're trespassing, Susie. That's not okay."

"But—"

"It's clear I'm going to have to install some cameras around here," he said, as much to himself as Susie. "Maybe even sit in my car out front some nights and see if I can catch whoever is doing this."

"No! Please!"

He stared at her. "Why not?"

"Because whoever my mystery visitor is, they're just trying to make a connection with someone. Why would we want to cut that off?"

"They can come by during business hours and connect," he protested.

She pointed his attention to the original note. "Remember this? 'I am a square peg too.' That means whoever this person is doesn't feel as if they fit in."

Brian read the same six words he'd seen the first day and then looked up at Susie, confusion etching fine lines along the outer corners of his warm brown eyes. "I'm not following the issue here."

"I wouldn't expect you would. You're—" She swept her hand at Brian's khaki slacks and short-sleeved collared shirt "—*normal*. But not everyone is."

"You lost me."

She didn't mean to laugh, but she couldn't help it as she commandeered the paper back from him and gave it a little shake. "My mystery visitor who is afraid to show his or her face, the teenage boy who couldn't walk his dog the other night without being teased about the size of his ears, the old man digging around in the dumpster last night... *Me*. We're all seen by the world as being somehow less."

"Wait. You?"

"Look at me." She pointed at her bow-tied braids, her elephant pants, and her ballet shoes. "Trust me, Brian, you don't have to pretend you don't think I'm odd. The world has let me know this since I was a little kid. And that's okay. I like bright, happy clothes. I like to surround myself with happy colors and hum happy songs. I'm okay with being a square peg. Really. But getting to where I am now wasn't always easy. There were days, weeks, even months, when I felt like such a hopeless outcast because of the way I am. Girls in school thought I dressed like a baby because I put bows in my hair every day in high school. Guys made snide comments in the hallway when I'd walk by in whatever flouncy dress I chose to wear while the other girls were in body-hugging yoga pants and crop tops. And when they heard the songs I tended to hum, the laughter was insane."

He rocked back on his heels, curious. "What kind of stuff did you hum?"

"It depended on what I was doing and feeling."

"Give me a for instance."

She glanced at her sunflower watch, noted the remaining five minutes before the market opened, and did a quick scan of her shelves to make sure she was ready. "I don't know… 'Singing in the Rain' on rainy days, 'Top of the World' when I got a good test grade or felt particularly happy for no apparent reason, and 'Jesus Loves Me' on hard days when I needed that reminder. All of those, as you know, are not the kind of music high schoolers are into. So my humming stuff like that just added to my freak points in everyone's eyes."

He blinked. She continued. "Then there was home. My parents are both doctors. My older sister is a lawyer. My brother started his own wildly successful tech company. And then there's me—Square

Peg Susie. Which, by the way, is my actual nickname in my family. But it fits."

Again, she looked at the shelves, the typewriter, and the birdhouse, and felt the joy they stirred deep inside her chest. "It fits me, *and* my booth."

"Susie, I think—"

She pointed at her watch. "It's nine o'clock, Brian. Time to open."

Chapter Five

"I imagine, based on that tune you're humming, you had another successful day?"

Susie glanced to her left and spotted Brian coming her way. Shifting the stack of boxes she'd nested inside one another to her left arm, she waited for him to catch up. "You know the song?"

"'Our God is an Awesome God.' By Rich Mullins, I believe."

She grinned. "Wow. Very nice. I'm impressed."

"Thanks. It's one of my favorites." He motioned to the boxes and, at her nod, took them from her arms. "So? Am I right? Another good day?"

"It was great. So many nice people, so many great conversations."

"And sales?"

"They were good too." They kept pace with one another down the sidewalk and across the curb to the car responsible for more than a few slowdowns from passing vehicles. "This is me. Or, rather, my car."

Brian stopped. "It...it looks like a ladybug. With"—he did a double take at the headlights—"eyelashes."

"I know, right? I love it." She felt inside her tote bag for the key and popped the trunk. "Did you know that ladybugs have two sets of wings?"

He pulled his attention off the car and fixed it, instead, on Susie. "I do now."

She took back the nested boxes, placed them in the trunk, and then closed it. "Also, not all ladybugs have spots. But I like them, so my ladybug car has them."

He glanced at the car and nodded. "It...works."

"Thanks." She stepped onto the curb and motioned down the sidewalk toward Main Street. "Anyway, I should probably start heading home. Have a nice evening, okay?"

He looked from Susie to the car and back again. "Aren't you forgetting something?"

She ran a quick mental inventory of everything she'd brought to the market that morning and everything she'd carried out and shook her head. "No, I'm pretty sure I have everything."

"Except your car," he said.

"I didn't forget that. I'd just rather walk now, while there's still some sun left in the sky, and then come get it later."

Again, he looked from Susie to the car and back again before stepping onto the sidewalk beside her with a lighthearted shrug. "Mind if I join you? There's a book I'd like to check out at the bookstore if they're still open."

"It's Tuesday. Book Club night. They're open until eight."

"Perfect."

Together, they made their way on foot to Peculiar's main thoroughfare, stopping every half block or so for Susie to point out a pair of birds or a particular flower or even a crack in the concrete that resembled the eastern border of the United States. Each time she did, Brian looked surprised, but soon he began asking follow-up

in Peculiar, Missouri

questions and, once or twice, even pointed out a few sightings of his own—like an empty swing swaying in the breeze and a tree branch that all but begged to be climbed.

A couple of blocks shy of Susie's, Brian's pace grew slower, his face reflective. "I can't tell you the last time I did this."

"Did what?" she asked.

"Walked. Looked. And noticed things." He stopped. "I mean, I've lived here my whole life, so I know this street, these houses. But I'm so used to it all, I don't really see it anymore, you know?"

Susie stopped too. "And I'm the complete opposite. I see everything—too much, sometimes."

"Meaning?"

"Well, imagine being my parent and having to get somewhere quickly. Only, I'm comparing cracks on the sidewalk to a country's border. It's too much sometimes. Was too much often."

He toed a tiny pebble between the edge of the sidewalk and a flower bed. "Maybe. For some, I guess. But I find it…and you…kind of refreshing, frankly."

An unfamiliar warmth spread across her cheeks and left her toeing at a different pebble while her gaze dropped to the ground and— "Oh, little one, I'm not going to hurt you," she said, dropping into a squat beside a ladybug. "I promise."

Bending down beside her, Brian followed her finger to a small red speck. "I'm pretty sure that ladybug is dead, Susie."

"Ladybugs often play dead when they feel threatened." Susie picked up the bug, set it down inside the flower bed, and gently stepped back onto the sidewalk. "Clearly my big foot was seen as danger."

Seconds later, the ladybug took flight onto a neighboring bush, and Susie smiled.

"You're something else, Susie Walker."

Her answering laugh earned a quick tweet from a passing bird. "That's a nice way of putting it."

He opened his mouth as if to speak but closed it as she resumed their walk, the lights of the Main Street shops growing closer with every step.

"I like this town," she said. "A lot."

"You do?"

Something about his voice made her glance in his direction, but when she did, his expression was unreadable. "I do. Like maybe I really don't have to consider being a hermit in order to be myself here."

"Trust me, you don't have to become a hermit. Not by a long shot."

Not sure what to make of his words, she redirected her attention to the sidewalk only to have him reclaim it again in short order. "That said, we do have a real live hermit in this town. He lives back there"—he pointed left, toward the trees on the north side of the town park—"deep in the woods."

"What's his name?" she asked.

Brian shrugged. "Folks around here call him Old Man Rogers."

"Have you ever seen him?"

"I saw his outline behind a curtain once when I was in high school. A few of my teammates from the football team dared me to ring his doorbell and see if he'd answer. He didn't, of course, but when we were running away, I looked back at his house. That's when I saw the outline of him standing behind the curtain."

"I see."

"Seeing him—or, rather, the outline of him—like that stuck with me. I tried to imagine what that would be like. To choose to stay in the same place, day after day, never interacting with people. Always being alone. In one place. I never went back after that. The other guys did, but I didn't."

"Why not?" she asked, studying him closely.

Brian shrugged. Shook his head. "I guess I felt like a jerk for invading his space like that. And for what? A few laughs? I mean, he keeps to himself for a reason, right? Who was I to mess with that?"

"If only more people could learn to be that respectful," she mused as they continued walking.

"I think I'm just a living, breathing example of what the pastor at my church often refers to as a work in progress or—"

She elbowed his sentence and their walk to an abrupt end. "Brian, look! It's almost exactly the same!"

Confused, he followed the path of her finger across the far edge of the park to a small work shed. Beside the shed was a bench. A few feet beyond the bench was a small birdbath, and a birdhouse hanging from the lowest branch of an oak tree. "What is?"

"The birdhouse! It's almost exactly like the one my mystery visitor left. Only that one, there, is pink with white gingerbread, and the one this morning was lavender with yellow gingerbread."

"Interesting." He motioned across the park. "Want to take a closer look?"

At her emphatic nod, they left the sidewalk, hurried across the recently mowed grass, and came to a stop beneath the near replica of the birdhouse she'd been taking inquiries about at her booth all day.

"Same porch, same window holes," she confirmed.

It was Brian's turn to nod. "Yup, I think it's safe to say that whoever made this birdhouse is one and the same as your mystery note leaver."

She walked in a circle under the birdhouse, chronicling everything about it one more time, and then, when she was satisfied Brian was right, turned her attention to the nondescript shed. "Who owns this shed?" she asked.

"The town. It's just a place for the maintenance crew to keep the equipment needed to care for the park—mower, weeder, blower, that sort of stuff," Brian explained. "They open it up when that stuff needs to be done and then close it back up until next time."

"Do you think one of them made the birdhouse?"

For a beat, maybe two, he said nothing as he considered her question, only to shake it off in the end. "I know all three guys on the town's maintenance crew. Played football with two of them, and my sister dated the other back in high school. I can't imagine any of them making something this intricate, let alone leaving the kind of notes you've been getting on your typewriter."

"Oh. Yeah. No, we're not talking about a former high school football player here…"

His laugh echoed around them. "What? Are you saying former jocks can't have a sensitive side?"

"No, I'm saying they're not the type to feel like an outsider." She paused, considered her words, and then held up her hands in surrender. "Actually, that's not fair. John 7:24 says I shouldn't judge based on appearance."

He shrugged. "True. But in this particular case, your assumption is more valid than not, I'm afraid."

in Peculiar, Missouri

She scanned their immediate surroundings, noting the playground to their left, a pair of shaded benches behind them, the shed to their right, and the woods ahead with the beginning of a footpath between thickly branched trees.

"Is that part of the park too?" she asked, pointing at the well-worn spot.

"Some of it, yes. The marked trails part. But if you venture off the paths, no." He led her to the entrance and held back one of the branches so she could view more of the path. "Which means they're not liable if you fall and crack your head should you choose to wander off the path. But, as you can see, it's heavily used. By hikers, joggers, high schoolers up to no good on a Friday night, et cetera, et cetera."

Like a balloon that met with a pinprick, she felt her whole body deflate. "Oh."

"Don't get discouraged just yet. *Someone* made those birdhouses." He let the branch fall back into place, gestured in the direction they'd come, and, at Susie's nod, fell into step beside her as they made their way across the grass to the sidewalk. "I'll call Matt first thing in the morning and see if he can tell me where they got the birdhouse. I would imagine he'll know something."

Hope drove her gaze up to Brian's face. A burst of shyness borne on the sweet expression she found there sent her gaze back down to her feet as they traveled the final block. "That would be really nice of you. Thank you."

"My pleasure." He slowed his pace as the sign for Peculiar Books grew closer. "It's not every day I get to help solve a mystery."

She laughed. "True."

"After I talk to him, do you want me to call you with what I find out?"

She took them past the bookstore's main door and stopped at the next. "I'd say yes if I had a phone, but I don't. So I guess you can just tell me on Thursday at the next market day?"

"You don't have a cell phone?" he asked.

"No."

"Or a landline?"

"At some point, I imagine I will. Maybe." Susie reached inside her tote, foraged around for her apartment key, and plucked it out. "I prefer to pass my time with music, books, and long walks rather than be tethered to a phone."

The shock on his face was palpable. "Then how do you keep in contact with friends or family in Connecticut?"

Laying a hand on his arm, she looked both ways, stepped closer, and lowered her voice to a whisper. "There's this thing called the mail. You write a letter, put it in an envelope with a stamp, and you pop it in a mailbox."

"Ha ha, smarty-pants."

She tried her best to bite back her smile, but it was no use. "Sorry. I couldn't resist. But, seriously, getting and sending letters is fun."

"What happens if you have an emergency or someone from home needs to reach you?" he countered.

"If I need to call them, I come down here, to the bookstore. And if someone from home needs to reach me, they have the bookstore's number."

He traveled the four or five steps back to the store's main entrance and tapped at the window placard detailing business hours. "And? If you have to make a call after hours?"

"I have a key for that." She folded her arms and leveled him with an amused expression. "You sound almost…*concerned*."

"Because I am."

The earnestness in his answer pushed her back a step. The confirmation evident in his eyes left her feeling adrift in waters she'd never encountered, let alone chartered. "I-I'm…it's fine. Really. It works for someone like me."

"Someone like you?"

Back on familiar land, she inserted the key into the lock and pushed open the door. "People tend not to look below my surface all that often, you know?"

"Then they're fools. Plain and simple."

Too stunned to speak, she said nothing.

"Well, thanks for letting me walk with you, Susie. It's been the best part of my day."

Turning, he headed back in the direction they'd come. Past Peculiar Books… Past the breakfast place… Humming.

Chapter Six

She'd just finished bagging her last customer's purchase when she spotted Brian making his way in her direction. A good half foot taller than her own five foot six inches, Brian was, without a doubt, a good-looking guy. Even without the short-sleeved shirt he wore, she knew his arms and his chest were toned in a way that spoke to physical labor and a history of athleticism. His generous lips were not the slightest bit shy about smiling, and, as he drew close enough to catch her looking at him, his chocolate-brown eyes crackled to life with a near heart-stopping warmth she couldn't ignore if she tried.

"Good day?" he asked. With those same eyes—they were still making it difficult for her to breathe—he slowly took stock of Susie. "If I'm not mistaken, I think this is the first time I've seen your hair down like that. It's really pretty."

She managed a quiet thank-you as his attention dropped to her flamingo-adorned tank top, her soft pink capris, and her white and pink wedge sandals. When he returned to her waiting gaze, he showed no sign of the disbelief or mocking amusement her choice of attire tended to elicit from people. Instead, she saw only happiness as he repeated his original question.

"It was a great day, actually," she managed around the odd lump that suddenly took up residence in her throat. "In fact, three of the people who bought my flavored fruit butters did so based on word of mouth from people I sold to on Saturday, so that's encouraging."

"Well, look at you. Only open for business three days, and people are already starting to seek you out."

Aware of her cheeks growing warmer from a combination of Brian—the man—and the genuineness of his praise, she cast about for a change of topic that would enable her to catch her breath. "Did you have a chance to call your friend on the town's maintenance crew? Matt, I think you said his name was?"

"I did, actually."

Intrigued, she leaned forward across the table between them. "And?"

"He has no idea where it came from. One day it was just hanging in the tree when he showed up to cut the grass. He saw it as an anonymous gift to the town and left it there. Said he and the other guys get inquiries about it all the time—people wondering who made it and how they can get one too." Brian's eyes led hers to the birdhouse now perched on a top shelf along the back wall of the booth. "Seems your mystery visitor could run a booth of their own if they wanted, with those birdhouses."

"Birdhouses, pencil boxes, and mailboxes," she corrected.

Brian frowned. "He left you a mailbox this time?"

"He or she. And yes, only it's not just any old mailbox." Susie motioned for him to step all the way into her booth. When he did, she led him to the trio of shelves lining the back wall and pointed to the top shelf on the left. "I can't tell you how many squeals that yielded today, and that's not counting my own when I found it beside the typewriter this morning."

Brian looked from Susie to the mailbox and back again, his brows knitted. "Was there another note too?"

"There was." She stepped over to the typewriter, reached behind it, and secured the sheet of paper that held her ongoing correspondence with the mystery visitor. "See? Tuesday evening, I left this…"

DON'T SELL YOURSELF, OR YOUR WOODWORKING TALENT, SHORT.
YOUR WORK IS BEAUTIFUL.
IF YOU WON'T SELL IT, MAY I SELL IT FOR YOU?

When Brian was done reading, she pointed below her words to the ones that had greeted her, along with the mailbox, that morning.

WHAT I LEAVE IS FOR YOU TO DO WITH AS YOU WILL.
IF IT BRINGS JOY TO SOMEONE, THAT IS REWARD ENOUGH FOR ME.

"I'm going to figure out a fair price and then add the things that have been left to my shelves come Saturday. Whatever money they make will be put aside for my mystery visitor."

She ran her finger across the detailing that made the mailbox appear as if it were a fish latching on to a baited lure. "It's almost inconceivable that someone with so much talent and ability can feel as if they don't belong or that they're not worthy of interacting with people, you know? Yet so many of us do."

"So many of *us*?" he echoed. At her nod, he stepped closer. "You interact with people all the time with your booth."

"I do. Because it's better than the alternative, and I've learned to accept myself as I am because God does. But not everyone is in that same place. Clearly this person—" She looked at the paper again and sighed. "Clearly this person isn't, and that's a shame."

A clench of defiance stiffened his jaw only to release on the heels of a heavy exhale. "Are you going to leave another note?"

"I am."

"Then I'll leave you to it. But stop by my office before you go, okay? I brought something for you."

Before she could question his words, Brian turned and made his way into the main aisle, his footfalls showing no sign of their earlier lightness as he headed in the direction of his office. When he disappeared from view, she fed the correct paper into the typewriter, readied her fingers on the keys, and began to type.

PERHAPS IT'S TIME TO TELL YOU A LITTLE ABOUT MYSELF.
MY NAME IS SUSIE.
SQUARE PEG SUSIE'S IS MY NEW BUSINESS.
IT'S A PLACE WHERE I CAN BE ME. QUIRKS AND ALL.
I MAKE AND SELL THINGS THAT MAKE ME HAPPY.
I WOULD LIKE TO BE YOUR FRIEND.

When she was done, she took a moment to reread her note, cleared a spot next to the typewriter for whatever the next item her mystery visitor might leave, and then gathered up her tote bag and headed for Brian's office. Along the way she passed Nate's Produce Stand, Stan's Rocking Chairs, Maura's Collectibles, and one booth still awaiting an occupant. While the market was quiet right now, everyone's business drew its share of customers during the nine-to-five window on Tuesdays, Thursdays, and Saturdays. Most of the vendors were friendly enough. They waved hello to Susie in the morning and goodbye as they headed home at the end of a busy day. A small handful—including Stan and Maura—enjoyed chatting with her during breaks in customers, but at the end of the day they hurried home to their respective families.

She'd hoped to find a friend or two at the market she could do things with on her off days and some evenings, but it was okay if she didn't. Simply being there, realizing her dream of owning her own business, was a big step. The rest, God willing, would follow in time.

At the doorway to Brian's office, Susie peeked inside, her gaze skirting the empty walls, the utilitarian-looking filing cabinet, the neatly stacked papers inside a wire basket on the desk, and, finally, Brian himself, seated behind the desk with the biggest sunflower she'd ever seen in his hands.

"Is that real?" she asked, pointing at the flower.

"It is."

She stepped into the room. "It's…incredible. Where did you find it?"

"I grow them out at my parents' farm." He stood and held the flower out for Susie to take. "I thought you might like this one."

"You… You brought me a-a flower?" she stammered.

"It made me think of you the second I saw it."

At a loss for what to say let alone how to act, she simply took the flower, her mouth agape.

"It seems, from what I've been able to gather, that yellow is one of your favorite colors. And your choice in watches seems to suggest you like sunflowers as well." Brian cleared his throat of its sudden rasp. "Plus, this one looked particularly happy and pretty. Like you."

She stumbled back a half step, certain she'd heard wrong. Before she could ask him to repeat himself, though, he locked his desk and dropped the key into the front right pocket of his pants. "I'm hoping, if you walked to work, that we could head into town together again this evening. I keep forgetting to pick up that book I've been wanting to get."

"I…uh…" She stopped and looked down at the flower then slowly lifted her gaze back to his. "That would be nice."

Wordlessly, they made their way out of the office, past the assortment of booths en route to the exit, and then turned, together, toward the heart of Peculiar, the only sound that of their respective footwear on the sidewalk beneath them.

"Your parents own a farm?" she finally asked even as her gaze remained riveted on the sunflower in her hand. "Here in Peculiar?"

"Yes. It's on the west side, near Wells Lake. It belonged to my grandparents when my grandfather was still alive. When he passed, my grandmother turned it over to my mom and my dad to run. I came on full-time after I graduated from college."

"Is the market a family thing as well?"

"Nope. The market is all me."

"Why?"

He slowed, pointed at a pair of cardinals playing tag in a nearby bush, and then motioned her onto a bench so they could watch while they spoke. "Do you mean why the market, or why all me?"

"I don't know." She shrugged. "Both, I guess?"

"Well, the market is a way to test my business instincts. And all me because I wanted to use some of the strengths and talents God has given me to accomplish something on my own, something that isn't mine simply by way of birthright."

She smiled as the birds continued their game, darting from one branch to the other. "I know I'm new, but from what I've seen so far, it seems like your business instincts are right on with the market. So many neat things under one roof."

"So far so good," he conceded. "The tricky part will be wintertime. People love open-air markets during the spring, summer, and fall. But when it's below freezing? I'm not so sure."

"I'll be game for trying."

"You might be singing a different tune when you see what winter is like out here."

"Trust me, Connecticut winters can get pretty dicey too, being on the East Coast. But space heaters are a marvelous invention. Or"—together, they watched the birds fly off—"maybe someone's got an empty barn you can rent for the coldest months."

In unison, they stood and resumed their journey. "Not a bad idea if someone would consider renting me space for four or five months," Brian mused.

"It would be more money than they'd get if it sat empty all twelve months, right?" Susie asked between sniffs of her flower.

"Good point. Definitely something worth checking into. Thanks."

Stopping, midstep, she waited for him to do the same. When he did, she met the questioning lift of his eyebrows with the smile he'd deserved back in his office. "Thank you for the flower. It's absolutely beautiful."

"I hoped you'd like it."

"I do. Very much. It was just unexpected, and something that's never happened to…" She shrugged again. "Anyway, I love it, and I know exactly where I'm going to put it when I get home."

"Oh?"

"On my front-facing windowsill. That way I can enjoy it, and so can the woman on the bench."

"Woman on the bench?" he echoed.

Susie pointed toward their destination and, at his nod, continued them on their way. "Yes. I don't know her name or even what she looks like beyond her gloved hands and her legs. But she sits on a bench across from my apartment door every morning, seemingly reading the paper."

"You don't think she's actually reading it?"

"I imagine she does. Some. But every time I step out my door either to go to work or just to start my day with a walk, I feel her looking at me. But the second I turn toward her, she hides behind her paper again, careful not to let me see her face."

Brian furrowed his brow. "Hmm. Okay, that's a little weird."

"Not really. People have been giving me double and triple takes for as long as I can remember. Which is why I'm assuming that getting a look at my choice in attire every morning has become sort of her routine, you know?"

"And you're okay with that?" he asked as they crossed the last block.

Susie laughed. "It's just the way it is, the way it's always been. So, yeah."

His pace noticeably slowed as they approached the bookstore, his eyes leading hers across Main Street to the now-empty bench across from her apartment door. "That's where she sits?"

"It is. Which is why my living room window will be the perfect place for my flower. It can brighten both of our days."

After a momentary glance up at the window in question, Brian lowered his full attention onto Susie, a tentative smile tugging at his lips. "You really are something else, Susie Walker. And not in the way you've been led to believe."

"I don't understand what you mean."

He released her gaze as he gestured to her sandals, her flamingo-inspired outfit, and, finally, the bright pink bow in her hair. "My grandmother has an expression for people like you. She calls them a breath of fresh air."

He shifted his weight from foot to foot, obviously uncomfortable yet refusing to let it deter him from a point he clearly wanted to make. "I never really knew what she meant by that until now. Or, more specifically, until you. I mean, it's like I said earlier… I thought of you when I saw that flower this morning. Because it made me happy. And honestly, being able to make people happy just by being yourself is a pretty special gift, if you ask me."

Too stunned to speak, Susie blinked. She looked down at her flower and then glanced back at Brian. "I—I don't know what to say to that," she whispered.

"I'm not looking for you to respond to what I said, Susie. Just hear it. Know it. And believe it." He hooked his thumb toward the bench. "Oh, and if you ask me, I'm going with a very different reason as to why this woman you mentioned parks herself on that bench

in Peculiar, Missouri

every morning. I think that seeing you being you makes her happy, Susie, just like it does me."

"But I—"

"I look forward to seeing you at the market again on Saturday." Walking backward past the bookstore, his answering smile reached straight to her heart. "Good night, Susie."

Chapter Seven

Hours slipped into days. Days slipped into a week. A week slipped into two. And, little by little, Susie began to feel as if Peculiar, Missouri, could, in fact, be her forever home.

Sure, she still saw her share of raised eyebrows when she walked down the street in her favorite polka-dotted rain boots on a sun-filled day. And, yes, she heard the snickers of her fellow twenty-somethings when she styled her hair in ponytails and secured them with brightly colored hair bows. But that would have been par for the course no matter where she chose to live.

What was different now, as opposed to her growing-up years, was that she finally had a chance to craft a life around her quirkiness rather than the other way around. True, her candles, pottery, and other homemade items would never make the kind of money her siblings stood to make with their careers, but they were selling. In fact, they were selling so well that the majority of her non-market days were spent molding clay, mixing scents, melting wax, and experimenting with various ribbons and hair fasteners. And while she did, she could sing or dance to her heart's content without worrying about embarrassing her parents if they were entertaining a friend or speaking with a client on a phone down the hall.

Best of all, though, was feeling like maybe, just maybe, she was actually making some real friends—people who not only seemed to

in Peculiar, Missouri

like her in spite of her oddities, but maybe even a few who actually embraced them as well.

People like Nate, from Nate's Produce Stand, who greeted her with a carefully selected piece of fruit matched to whatever color she'd chosen to wear on that particular market day.

Or like Stan, from Stan's Rocking Chairs, whose waiting smile was always followed by some sort of endearment spoken in his native Italian. He would translate so Susie could understand and then beam with pride when she'd take the time to repeat it back to him as he'd originally said it.

And like Maura, from Maura's Collectibles, who routinely spent her limited lunch break stopping by to chat and often sent customers Susie's way.

And her mystery visitor, who still had not shared his or her name yet, welcomed Susie to work on market mornings with a kind note and the latest in a growing list of fast-selling wood-crafted pieces.

And, of course, like Brian—the handsome former high school athlete who walked her home at the end of every market day under the guise of needing to stop by Peculiar Books yet always left without ever going inside.

Truth be told, their walks were something she'd come to look forward to—the pace, the rhythm, the conversation, and even the moments when there was no conversation at all. Most days she knew they were just two people of similar age spending a little time together. But sometimes—when Susie let Maura get in her head—she wondered if maybe he really did like her as more than a friend.

Was it possible?

Could someone like Brian Bonner—a guy who'd fit in everywhere his entire life—be interested in someone nicknamed Square Peg Susie?

She shook the ludicrous thought from her head and set Nate's perfectly ripened banana, matched to her yellow dress, on her booth's front table, glanced over at the spot where her mystery visitor always left the day's mystery item, and felt the answering sag of her body at its emptiness. Crossing to the typewriter, Susie looked down at the most recent message she left and the stark, white nothingness directly below it.

A cold chill worked its way along her spine as she, again, looked at the same spot where she'd found the pencil box, the birdhouse, the mailbox, the Square Peg Susie's sign that now hung above her booth, the stick pony, the fairy house, and, most recently, the picture frame. Yet unlike all those other market mornings, there was nothing.

No item.

No note.

No sign anyone had been anywhere inside—

"Good morning, Susie."

Glancing over her shoulder, Susie searched for the face that matched the voice. Sure enough, she found Brian standing just inside her booth with two to-go cups nestled in a carton in his left hand and a small white paper bag in his right hand. "Something is very wrong, Brian."

"What?" He set the carton and bag on the front table and hurried over to her. "What's wrong?"

"My mystery visitor..." She swept her hand toward the typewriter and the empty surface to its right. "For the first time since I opened my booth for business, there's no note on the typewriter and no wooden piece."

"So they really didn't show, after all... Interesting."

She slid her fingers across the typewriter's center keys as she took in the words she'd typed before leaving work on Thursday.

I'M MEETING NICE PEOPLE HERE. REAL FRIENDS PERHAPS.
THEY ARE PEOPLE I WORK ALONGSIDE HERE AT THE MARKET.
I KNOW IT'S NOT ALWAYS EASY BEING DIFFERENT.
BUT NOT EVERYBODY SHUTS US OUT BECAUSE OF IT.

"We've been having a really nice back-and-forth this last week. Like maybe I'm making progress in helping him or her feel less alone. But now..." Dropping her hand, Susie leaned her shoulder against the nearest shelf and sighed. "I don't know what to think."

Brian peeked around the rear bank of shelves, looked at the typewriter, and then pointed her back to the front table. "If it'll help, I picked up a hot chocolate and a slice of apple crumb bread for you on the way through town this morning."

A knowing cough from the direction of Maura's booth let Susie know she wasn't dreaming. Yet, still... "You—you brought me a drink?" she echoed.

"And the best apple crumb bread ever." He reached inside the bag, extracted a slice of bread, and handed it, along with one of the to-go cups, to a gaping Susie. "Trust me, you'll love them both. Wendy at Peculiar Bakery is a baking master. Even flavors I don't normally like taste good in whatever she makes because—wait... Why do you look like you're going to cry all of a sudden?"

Shaking her head, she looked from the slice of bread to Brian and back again. "I'm okay. Really. I'm just not accustomed to someone doing something like this for me. I've never had anyone bring..." She stopped, drew in a steadying breath, and then found the smile the man and his unexpected kindness deserved. "Thank you. Truly. It's a lovely surprise."

"You're welcome." He lifted his own slice of apple crumb bread as if in a toast and then took a bite. "Mmm... So good. So very, very good."

She tried a bite, traded knowing smiles with Brian, and then nudged her chin back to the typewriter and the blank spot where her mystery visitor's latest reply should have been. "Why didn't they come this time?"

"It rained pretty hard last night," Brian suggested between sips of his hot beverage.

"Last week's rain didn't stop whoever this is from coming then."

Brian took another bite of bread and chased it down with a longer sip of his drink. "Maybe they weren't feeling well? Maybe they didn't have a new item to leave? Maybe—"

"Maybe the note I left felt too much like pressure?" Susie mused. "And, thus, scared them off?"

"If he or she didn't see it, it couldn't scare them off, right?"

Susie considered his words as she took a sip of her hot chocolate. "But there's no way of knowing it wasn't seen."

"That's not necessarily true." He picked a stray breadcrumb off his shirt and popped it into his mouth. "I mean, at the time, I just figured I missed him. But, considering this is the first time there was no response on the typewriter and no gift left, I think it's safe to say that my watching from the car last night spooked him—*or her*—off."

She stared at Brian across the top of her to-go cup. "You were outside the market last night? Watching for my mystery visitor?"

Beaming, he nodded. "I thought it was time we figured out who it was, you know? And camping outside the entrance in my car for a few hours was a cheaper way to do it than installing security cameras. That is, if it had actually worked, of course."

"How could you do that?" she countered.

"It was easy." He finished his drink and stuffed the cup inside the same bag that had held both slices of bread upon his arrival. "I waited until after sunset, grabbed a book, headed over here, and waited. In fact, it's because of the book I figured I missed him. But now, knowing there is no note, I'm guessing I didn't. Or if I did, it was the moment he or she spotted me sitting in the car and decided to turn around and leave."

She put down the cup and the rest of her slice and folded her arms across her smocked dress. "I asked you not to do that."

His smile fading, he drew back. "You asked me not to use a camera, and I didn't. But I thought you'd want to finally know who's been leaving these notes and things."

"I do. But only in the right way."

"And what do you consider the right way?"

"When my mystery visitor *wants* me to know."

"You're angry."

Was she? Powered by a slew of emotions she found difficult to corral, she paced between the typewriter and Brian. Once. Twice.

"Not everyone is as confident in themselves as you are, Brian. Not everyone is comfortable everywhere they go. It takes effort and courage for people like us."

"Us? Who's us?"

She stopped. Blew out a breath. "People like the woman who watches me from the bench outside my apartment every morning. People like the boy in the park who's ridiculed by other kids just because his ears are bigger than"—she hooked her fingers in the air—"*normal*. People like the elderly gentleman who dumpster-dives in the alley behind my apartment. People like my mystery visitor who clearly feels like he or she doesn't fit in this world. And, yes, people like me who prefer to do things a little differently than everyone else.

"You've always been popular. That's obvious every time I see people approach you or slow their car down just so they can say hi. You were on the high school football team. Your family grew up here. Their family before them lived here. It's different for you."

Now that she was going, she didn't know how to stop. It was as if a dam she'd built up over her twenty-five years of existence had finally given way. "All my life I was the outcast. The one the kids in school whispered about the second I got on the school bus or walked in the door. The one whose family is made up of people who are all eerily similar except for the one odd duck—the one everyone else jokes about being adopted or from another planet or part of some scientific experiment gone wrong.

"But I'm not any of those things. I wasn't adopted, I'm just different. I'm not a freak or lacking fashion sense, I just like what I like. Because here's the thing. I'm *me*. Just like all the other misfits are just them. Are we square pegs? Sure. But we're still pegs, Brian. Pegs that God fearfully and wonderfully made."

"Susie, I..." Brian raked his hands through his hair. "I don't know what to say. Technically, I have every right to find out who is coming into my market after hours and messing around in one of my vendors' booths. But I let go of that right when it became clear they meant no harm and that you didn't mind. Still, I think it's only natural that I'd be curious who it is."

"But don't you see? This thing that you're merely curious about is something much bigger for the person who's been typing these notes and leaving these things. For *that* person, this has been a way to connect. A way to interact with someone in a way that felt safe. A place to get validation for an ability they're too shy to share with the world as the person they are. An opportunity to feel as if someone looked forward to interacting with them."

Brian shook his head. "And I drove them away."

Unable to soften the truth in his words, Susie shrugged.

"Great." Fixing his gaze on a spot just north of her head, Brian shook his head again. "I'm sorry, Susie. I really am. I thought it would be fun to solve the mystery and—"

"Excuse me, miss? Can I get some help?"

Stepping to the left, Susie looked past Brian to the elderly woman standing in front of a wire shelf holding a pair of lavender-scented candles in her age-spotted hands. "Of course."

Turning back to Brian, Susie drew in a breath, held it for a beat, and then slowly let it out. "Duty calls, I'm afraid."

"No worries. I won't keep you any longer." He grabbed the bag containing his empty cup and headed for the exit. When he reached it, he turned back to Susie, all signs of the joy and lightness he'd arrived with now gone. "Please know, though, that I'm not about intentionally hurting people. It's not how I was raised to be, and it's not how I've chosen to live my life. Yet here I am, having done exactly that—to this mystery visitor, and to you. And for that, I'm truly, truly sorry."

Before she could respond, he nodded at the candle-holding customer, tossed the white paper bag into the trash receptacle just outside Susie's booth, and then disappeared into the rapidly growing market-day crowd.

Chapter Eight

"Brian?"

Looking up from his calculator, the brains behind Bonner's Open-Air Market noted Susie's presence with a single nod and a brief glance at the wall clock opposite his desk. "You heading out?" he asked, his voice void of its usual animation.

"I am, but—" She stepped all the way into the small office. "I hoped we could talk."

When he made no move to stand or gather his stuff so he could walk with her as they'd been doing for nearly two weeks, she pointed to the empty chair to the left of the desk. "May I sit for a moment?"

He leaned back in his chair, tented his fingers, and offered a slow nod.

"I want to apologize for getting so upset with you this morning," she said. "It wasn't right, and it wasn't fair."

Relief traded places with wariness as Brian pitched forward. "No, no, it's okay. You were right. I've never felt like an outcast in school, at home, or in my adult life. It's why I didn't understand what was wrong with sitting outside in my car, waiting for your mystery visitor to show up. But after what you said, I get it. Or, at least, I'm trying to get it. Either way, though, it's done, and I don't know how to fix it. And I don't know how to make it so you don't think I'm a first-class jerk."

She didn't mean to laugh. But the release of tension that came with it was sorely needed. "Trust me, Brian, I don't think you're a jerk. First-class, or otherwise."

"I'm sensing a *but*..."

"Not a but, per se, but..." Grinning, she rolled her eyes. "Oops. Sorry."

It was Brian's turn to laugh. "Carry on."

"What I'm trying to say is, I know you weren't trying to hurt anyone and I'd like a chance to help you understand why I got so upset over someone I've never met."

His laughter stopped, but his smile continued. "I already understand, Susie. I've been seeing the why since the first time we walked back to your place together. You care about people and animals and trees and bugs and everything around you. It's what makes you so unique and so hard to get out of my—"

Shifting quickly in his seat, he waved aside the rest of his sentence. "Anyway, we're good then?"

"We're good." Susie stood and motioned to the door. "Well then, I guess I should leave you to your calculations."

"Please don't," he said, shoving the calculator to the side. "I'd much prefer to walk you to your place just like normal. Assuming you're good with that, of course."

She bit back her answering smile and, instead, playfully moved her head as if weighing something. "Are you going to go inside the bookstore and pick up your book this time?"

"Ahhh... The book... Right... I keep forgetting that, don't I?"

"Yes."

"Well, I guess we'll just have to see if I remember this time." He stood, locked the top drawer of his desk, and then guided her out of his office and into the lingering warmth of the June evening.

Together, they made their way over to the sidewalk that bordered the eastern side of Main Street and headed south, their feet agreeing on an acceptable pace in short order. For a block, maybe two, she tried to keep it light, to talk about her day and ask about his, to draw his attention to birds and sounds. But then she decided to confide in him even further.

"Not everyone like me is as lucky as I've been," she said. "Yes, my family nicknamed me Square Peg long before I hit kindergarten, but it wasn't in a way to tear me down. They were just being honest. I did weird stuff. I liked weird stuff. I played weird stuff. But they never tried to change me, never tried to shame me into being normal even when it would've been the easier thing to do.

"Instead, when I'd come home crying because some bully told me I was stupid for saving an ant, or some girl I'd always thought was my friend found my choice in clothes so embarrassing she refused to sit with me at lunch, my mom would just wipe my tears and remind me that I was loved. Exactly the way I was. By her. By my dad. By my family. And, most of all, by God. She said it every single time. Which, during the middle and high school years, was pretty much nightly. But I'm so glad she did, because those words became my own personal North Star, allowing me to keep my head down until I was on the other side of those years."

She stopped, inhaled the lilac-scented air, and continued on, baring her soul to this man who made her feel like she could. "It wasn't until college was behind me and I was poised to really start my own life that I realized I didn't want to have to keep my head down. I wanted to hold my head up high and be me—a person who doesn't think ponytails and hair bows are just for kids, who wants to wear rain boots because I like them, who thinks it's okay to dance down the sidewalk if the mood strikes, who thinks those childhood stands to make money can be adultified, and who thinks kindness should be a given.

"And that's when I started looking online. To see if maybe there was a place I might fit better. Where I would have to learn to pick myself up rather than always leaning on my mom. Where I could forge my own path and dance my way down it every day if I wanted to. And that's when I came across a letter to the editor printed in *The Peculiar Times* ten years ago."

"Wait." Brian sped up enough to be able to stop in front of Susie. "You're telling me that some old letter you found online convinced you to up and move halfway across the country? To this place?"

"Yep." She nudged him forward and onto the next block, the sound of their steps against the concrete fading against that of her voice once again. "That's what I'm saying. And yes, most of my family thought I was nuts too. But when, on the third try, I was finally able to read the letter aloud to my mom from start to finish without crying, she understood enough to give me her blessing."

"And here you are."

"And here I am," she agreed.

"Any regrets so far?"

"Not a one." She stopped talking long enough to point at a bird foraging for worms in a freshly mulched flower bed. When the bird took flight with its captured prey, they resumed their walk. "But that's because my mom's encouragement all those years gave me the air I needed to come here. To the place I'd read about. And because I did, I've been able to follow my dream of opening my own business, I'm able to make my home exactly the way I want it, and I think I might be on the road to actually making some real honest-to-goodness friends.

"Are there still people who gawk at me? Sure. I see it all the time. But it's easier to shrug off when I feel connected in other areas. Clearly, my mystery visitor doesn't feel that. And clearly, he or she doesn't have someone like my mom to boost them up and remind them of God's love. So that's what I wanted to be for them. And I failed."

Brian blew out a breath of frustration. "You didn't fail, Susie. This mystery visitor was connecting with you. Right up until I ruined it last night by trying to play undercover detective."

"Maybe it really was the rain and not you at all," she said as they covered the last one hundred feet or so to the bookstore and her apartment's ground-floor entrance.

"Do you really believe that?"

"Can I plead the Fifth?" she asked as she reached into her tote bag and pulled out her key.

"I'm really sorry, Susie."

"I know. And so am I for getting so upset. But maybe everything I just shared with you can help you understand why I did. Right or wrong, I feel my mystery visitor's pain, and I want to do whatever I can to make them feel like they belong here."

"Just like you."

She inserted the key in the lock but stopped short of actually turning the knob. "Yes," she said, grinning. "Just like me. Soon."

"Not soon. *Now*."

"Thank you."

"I'm only speaking the truth as I see it." He lifted his hand as a shield against the evening sun. "For what it's worth, I'm going to go home and see if I can find this letter you talked about online. Sounds like it's something worth reading."

"You'd like to read it?" Susie asked.

"Sure."

"C'mon then." She pushed open her door and motioned him to follow her inside. "I have it upstairs in my apartment. In a frame."

"You framed it?" he echoed.

"It's a special letter."

He looked from Susie to the staircase beyond and then back to Susie. "If it brought you here, then yeah, I have to agree."

Unsure of how best to respond, Susie opted to simply lead the way upstairs to the landing she'd spent hours painting over the past few days. "Please excuse the smell of paint. I aired the stairwell out as best I could yesterday, but since I was at the market all day today, I had to close it up again."

"You did this?" Brian asked, staring at the wall directly in front of him. At Susie's nod, he moved in for a closer look. "The grass… It looks so real. Like I could just pluck out that blade right there and—is that a fairy?"

"It is. And yes, I painted this. My landlord, Marge, said I could."

in Peculiar, Missouri

He bent over to take in a caterpillar at the base of a tree and whistled long and low when he did. "Susie, this is incredible. How did you learn to paint like this?"

"I didn't have a lot of friends, remember?" She took in her efforts, mentally noted the perfect spot to add a ladybug, and then pushed open the door to her small yet cozy new home. "Fair warning, my love for color extends beyond my wardrobe."

"No warning necessary." He stepped all the way into her living room and slowly turned in a circle, drinking in every detail from the sky-blue curtains to the throw pillows that looked like snippets of sky against the futon's cream-colored cushion. "This is really cool."

"It's not magazine chic, but it makes me happy."

He took one last look around before meeting and holding her gaze. "It makes me happy too. It's like—wait… You have a speck of glitter right here." He ran the pad of his thumb gently across her forehead. "Got it."

"It's fairy dust, actually. And you'll find it sprinkled everywhere in here. In fact, you've got some on you already and"—she ran her index finger across his chin—"I got it too."

"Fairy dust?"

"That's right." She shrugged. "Anyway, you said you'd like to read the letter to the editor that brought me here." At Brian's nod, she led him back to the scrap of parquet flooring that denoted the apartment's foyer and pointed at the framed printout on the wall to the left of the door. "In light of the fact this was written ten years ago, I had to settle for printing it off my computer. But that's okay. Having it on real newsprint wouldn't change the words, right?"

"Right."

She followed his eyes to the sky-blue frame and the letter that had brought her to this place and this new life.

Dear Editor,

Before I moved to Peculiar more than sixty years ago, I longed for a place that would feel like a home should feel. A place where I was seen and appreciated for who I was, not who or what I wasn't. Because until I came here, that wasn't the case.

The woman you've all embraced despite her crazy height and propensity for losing herself among her potted plants was once seen as being nothing special. I wasn't particularly pretty, I spurted up to six feet tall in middle school, and I preferred plants over my peers. I was as grey as my name, they said.

Unfortunately, when you hear something enough, you start to believe it. That's the danger in being cruel, in being unwelcoming, in judging people by some made-up barometer of what should and shouldn't be.

That all changed, though, when I came here. People saw past the things that had always made me different and opted to focus, instead, on my heart and soul—two things I'd started to lose sight of all those years ago.

So thank you, Peculiarites. For helping me find real joy, true peace, life-changing love, and, last but not least, myself.

Sixty years ago, I came here because it was somewhere to go.

Today, it's the only place I want to be.

With deep gratitude,

Rhoda Grey Oaks

"Rhoda Grey Oaks?" Brian said, drawing back. "This says Rhoda Grey Oaks…"

Susie smiled, her gaze moving between the letter and the man now staring at her, wide-eyed. "That's right. She's the person who wrote the letter. Do you know her?"

"That's my grandmother!"

Chapter Nine

Susie was waiting outside her apartment door at nine o'clock the next morning when Brian pulled up to the curb in his mud-spattered pickup truck and hopped out onto the street.

"Good morning, Susie." He crossed the sidewalk and hurried to open the passenger door. "Excited to meet Nana?"

"Oh yes," she said as she slid onto the bench seat. "Nervous too."

When she and her skirt's hem were safely inside, he closed the door and smiled at her through the open window. "Don't be nervous. Nana is the best. I promise."

"If you say so."

He patted the top of his truck. "I do."

Smoothing her skirt, she waited as he crossed back to the driver's side and took his place behind the wheel. Before he piloted them away from the curb, though, he nudged his chin and her attention to the bench on the other side of the street. As he did, its occupant quickly straightened the newspaper she was reading so as to shield her face from view. "Is that the one you've told me about? The one you think is watching you?"

"It is."

"What's with the gloves?" he asked. "It's June."

Susie shrugged.

"Do you know how long she's been there?"

"Since I left for my morning walk just after sunrise."

"It's like the second she saw me glance her way, she shifted that paper so I couldn't see her."

"That's what she does."

He ping-ponged his eyes between Susie and the bench for a moment. "Have you thought about going over and asking what she's doing and why?"

"No. If she wanted to engage me in conversation, she would. Clearly, she doesn't want to."

He started to say something only to shake his head, shift the truck into drive, and pull onto the street, heading north. A block or so past her apartment, he glanced her way. "Those are my favorites," he said, leading her gaze down to her rain boots. "The little chicks are so subtle you might mistake them as straight-up polka dots if you're not paying attention."

"You don't think it's odd that I wear rain boots when it's sunny?"

"It caught me by surprise the first time or two, but now it's just…*you*." At the first four-way stop they came to, he turned west, skirting them past neighborhoods of small homes and neighborhoods of larger homes before giving way to wider spaces inhabited only by trees. "That said, as you can probably tell by my truck, the rain we've been having lately is making for some mud out at the farm. I'll try to keep you out of those areas so your boots don't get messed up."

Smiling, she looked out at the passing woods. "If they do, they do. That's the beauty of rain boots. They clean easily."

The wind through their opened windows carried his laugh. "You're a glass-half-full kind of person, I see."

"I guess I am." She pointed at the approaching change in landscape that soon had the forest bowing to a split-rail fence that bordered a large tract of land. A white clapboard sign bore the name, GREY-OAKS FARM. In the fields closest to the road, she saw strawberry plants, and in the fields beyond, corn. "Oh Brian, this is beautiful."

"Thank you. We'll keep it," he said, grinning.

"It looks like a lot of land."

"That's because it was actually two farms before my maternal grandparents married. Oaks Farm was in my grandfather's family, and James Farm was what my grandmother's farm was called when she first took it over from her uncle. Eventually Nana changed it to Grey Farm in honor of her maiden name and family, and then, when she and my grandfather got married, they merged the two farms into what you see today."

Susie straightened in her spot, drinking in the beginning edge of the farmhouse she could see from the road. Tucked behind it, beside the most spectacular climbing tree she'd ever seen, was a smaller house. "Who lives there?" she asked, pointing.

"That would be Nana. She and my grandfather had the smaller house built for themselves when they got serious about turning the farm over to my parents shortly after I was born. At the same time, they turned the house across the street into farmhand quarters. Of course, with Nana and Gramps being Nana and Gramps, they both stayed active in the day-to-day operations of the farm right up until Gramps passed eleven years ago. Even now, though, I still come across Nana out in the fields doing things she shouldn't be doing at eighty-six years old."

in Peculiar, Missouri

She hung on his every word, listening to and digesting it all as he turned onto the one-lane dirt road leading to both houses. "Oh, you have a barn!" she said, leaning forward in her seat. "Any animals?"

"Actually, there were two barns originally. One for each farm. But when Gramps and Nana decided to build the smaller house for themselves, they opted to put it where the Oaks barn was." He slowed the truck to a near crawl to accommodate a number of rain-induced ruts. "As for animals? There weren't, originally. But when I was a kid, Gramps got me a pair of goats and a few chickens to take care of and, well, the kids and grandkids of that first pair of goats are living life here on the farm."

"And the chickens?" she asked.

"They and their offspring and their offspring's offspring have been providing us with fresh eggs for breakfast ever since." Slowly, they bumped their way past the main house before stopping beneath the climbing tree to the side of the smaller house. "So? Are you ready to meet the woman who brought you here to Peculiar?"

Wiping her hands on her skirt, Susie shook her head. "I'm nervous again."

"Why?" he asked as he shut down the truck. "Nana's great."

"I have no doubt about that, based on her letter. But…" She gazed at the walkway to the front door. "She's why I'm here, Brian. Why I packed up my life and came here. And now? I'm getting to meet her."

Brian laughed. "She's not a celebrity."

"She is to me," Susie replied, her voice barely more than a whisper.

His hand closed over hers. Squeezed. "C'mon. She's gonna love you."

Before she could come up with a reason to stall, Brian pushed open his door, hurried around to her side, and waited as she exited the truck. Then, together, they followed the walkway to the front porch and the screen door beyond.

"Nana?" he called, knocking on the doorframe. "You here?"

When there was no answer, he knocked again. "Nana?"

"Maybe she went out—"

"No. She's here." Cocking his head, Brian held up his finger, crossed to the far side of the porch, and leaned across its upper railing. "Nana? What are you doing? I told you I'd get to those weeds this afternoon."

"I wanted to get to them now."

Brian turned back to Susie, shrugged an impish smile, and then returned to hanging over the railing once again. "Nana, can you please stop that for now? I brought someone to meet you, and it'd be a lot nicer for you to talk to her inside rather than—"

Susie stepped off the porch, followed it around to the far side of the house, and came to a stop beside a wrought-iron bench nestled among a grove of sunflowers. "Oh! This is absolutely beautiful."

Eyes the color of a summer sky peeked out from around a cluster of flowers, studied Susie from her bright yellow hair bow down to her polka-chick rain boots, and then slanted her attention back to her grandson. "Who is this ray of sunshine, young man?"

Susie stepped forward, her hand extended. "I'm Susie. Susie Walker. I moved to Peculiar from Connecticut a few weeks ago. Because of you."

in Peculiar, Missouri

Rhoda Oaks released Susie's hand and struggled onto her feet with the help of a simple wooden cane. "Because of *me*?"

"Yes." Susie accepted the woman's invitation to join her on the bench and, when they were settled side by side, turned just enough to afford them eye-to-eye contact. "You made me feel like maybe there might actually be a place where I could be me and that would be okay."

"How in the world did I do that, dear?" Rhoda asked, not unkindly.

"I don't remember what happened the day I found it. I don't remember if someone had said something hurtful, or if I was just tired of being a square peg in my own life, or what it was. But I had this overwhelming need for a place where I could be me and, as I said earlier, be okay doing so. So I got on my computer and started searching towns in all sorts of different ways. And then, all of a sudden, I came across a letter to the editor of *The Peculiar Times* that you wrote ten years ago."

Rhoda's blue eyes rounded with shock. "You found my letter on the computer? How did it get there?"

Swinging his legs over the railing, Brian hopped to the ground. "*The Peculiar Times* is also virtual these days, Nana. Has been for more than a decade. So that's how Susie was able to find your letter despite her being in Connecticut."

"I cried when I read it," Susie admitted. "As in, full-on tears."

Rhoda drew back in horror. "Why?"

"Because I identified with what you wrote. And, for the first time, I thought maybe there really was a place I could go. The same place you went sixty years ago," Susie said.

"And so you moved here? Because of my letter?"

Susie's emphatic nod earned a knowing smile from Brian and another round of shock from Rhoda. "I read it again and again and, when I knew what I needed to do, I read it to my mom. The moment she gave me her blessing, I started planning my move and found an apartment."

"She's living in the apartment above the bookstore, Nana," Brian interjected before motioning for Susie to continue.

"And I found Brian's market during a late-night search for ways I could open a little shop."

Rhoda looked from Susie to her grandson and back again. Waiting.

"When I got here, I filled out the necessary forms to rent booth space from Brian, and I opened Square Peg Susie's."

"It's becoming quite the draw too," Brian added. "I'm constantly being asked to point the way to Susie's booth."

Rhoda shot her hands up in a request for quiet. "Square Peg Susie's?"

"Yes. I named my shop in honor of my childhood nickname."

"People called you Square Peg Susie?"

Susie smiled. "Mostly just my family, but yes."

"Your family..."

"Yes." At the flash of indignation in the elderly woman's eyes, Susie shook her head, still smiling. "It's okay. I didn't mind it. Really. I've never doubted my family's love. But the fact is that I am...different. I"—she swept her hand from the top of her head to the tips of her boots—"dress like this all the time. And while most girls outgrow the hair bow phase by the time they go to second grade, I held on to it, along with wearing pigtails and braids. Not because I'm trying to be five, but because I don't think that kind of joy is something you have to outgrow in the name of normalcy."

"And the rain boots?" Rhoda asked, leaning down for a closer look. "Wait. Are those polka dots baby chicks?"

"Yes, they are," Susie and Brian said in unison.

"They're adorable."

Susie's face flushed warm at Rhoda's kindness. "Thank you."

"You're considered a square peg because you dress differently?" Rhoda asked, lifting her gaze back to Susie's.

"No, it's more than that. I'm just different. Always have been. I was the kid who couldn't kill a spider, the girl who didn't mind getting messy, the woman who paints a fairy meadow on the wall outside her apartment, etcetera."

Understanding made its way across Rhoda's gently lined face. "And you found a letter written by me—the too-tall woman who preferred plants over peers and whose last name fit the way the world saw me before I came to Peculiar."

Overcome by a rush of emotion, Susie looked down and swallowed. "That's right."

Crossing his arms, Brian leaned back against the porch railing. "If you ask me, Susie is exactly what you described her as right out of the gate, Nana. A ray of sunshine. And not just because she often dresses in yellow from head to toe. It radiates out of her in everything she does and says too."

Rhoda looked over at Brian but remained silent as he continued. "She's also an unbelievably talented painter and has the kindest heart of anyone I've ever met. This person—we call 'the mystery visitor'—has been leaving Susie notes on the typewriter she keeps in her booth. Or at least they did until yesterday. It's someone who sees themselves as a square peg too. We don't know if this person is a male or female, but we know that he or she has an amazing talent with woodworking. Along with the note left on the typewriter, there's always some sort of handcrafted wooden item left behind. Susie asked permission to sell them, and she's been saving the money made by this mystery visitor ever since."

"Why no note or item yesterday?" Rhoda asked, clearly intrigued.

Susie started to answer but stopped when Brian pushed off the railing and made his way over to the area his grandmother had been weeding. "When the note and item showed up on Susie's first day at the market, I was concerned. I didn't like the idea of someone coming into the market after hours, for obvious reasons. But Susie convinced me to let it go when it became apparent this person had no ill intentions. Eventually, though, I got caught up in the mystery of who was doing this. So I sat in my car outside the market entrance the night before last, hoping to finally figure out who the mystery visitor was."

Rhoda's gasp echoed around them. "Oh, Brian... You scared them off."

"I sure did." Brian squatted down beside a weed and yanked it from the ground. "And trust me, Nana, I realize the mistake I made in doing that, and I feel awful about it."

"You have no idea who it is?" Rhoda asked, swinging her attention back to Susie.

Susie shook her head. "No, and I don't think they want me to know."

"Then you have to respect that."

"I know. Because if I don't, I stand to lose whatever connection we've forged—a connection this person clearly wants and needs." Susie stood, wandered between a trio of sunflowers, and gently ran her fingers across their many petals. "But their woodworking abilities have made them a nice sum of money that is rightfully theirs. And I want to be their friend whether anyone else does or not."

A blanket of silence fell across the garden as Rhoda took off her gardening gloves and rested them beside her on the stone bench. Then, with the help of her cane, she rose and beckoned her grandson and Susie to come close.

"May I make a suggestion in regards to your mystery visitor?" she asked.

Susie and Brian traded glances before focusing on Rhoda once again. "Of course," Susie said.

"Instead of trying to figure out who it is"—Rhoda eyed her grandson before looking back at Susie—"or worrying about getting money to them, perhaps the best thing to do is simply concentrate on spreading kindness where it appears most needed. Maybe, in doing that, the truth will reveal itself in the end."

Again, Brian and Susie traded glances, with Brian breaking it in favor of his grandmother. "And if it doesn't reveal itself in the way we want it to?"

"Then it doesn't, right?" Susie said, looking at Rhoda. "Either way, though, you can't go wrong spreading kindness."

Beaming, Rhoda took hold of Susie's hands and gently squeezed. "Sixty years ago, Brian's grandfather encouraged me to write a letter telling the people of Peculiar how much their warm embrace changed my life. I started that letter but never finished it, never did anything with it. Then, ten years ago, after Martin passed, I came across that original draft while going through some of our things. Armed with fifty more years of living in this town at that point, I decided to sit down, start over from scratch, and actually finish it once and for all. When I was done, before I could get cold feet, I sent it off to the newspaper."

"And I'm so very glad you did," Susie said, returning the squeeze. "Without that letter, I wouldn't be here right now."

Rhoda abandoned her view of Susie in favor of her grandson, and her gaze lingered for a few beats. "Then I'm glad I did as well, young lady. Very glad, indeed."

Chapter Ten

"You've been mighty quiet since we left the farm." Brian shifted his pickup truck into park and turned to Susie. "Those new baby goats tucker you out?"

Leaning her head back, Susie smiled. "They were so, so cute. Especially the one you call Mighty Max."

"Ahhh…Mighty Max. He's definitely a character," Brian said, laughing. "He sure did take a shine to you. Would've climbed right up in the truck with you if his legs had been a little longer, huh?"

"I wouldn't have minded."

"*You* might not have, but I suspect Marge wouldn't have been too crazy about having a goat as a tenant."

Her answering laugh mingled with Brian's for a moment only to fade as her thoughts wandered away from the barn and the medley of animals she'd met and sent her gaze skittering to the opposite side of the street. "Maybe she's not watching me at all. Maybe she's waiting for me to talk to her because she's lonely."

"She?"

"The woman behind the newspaper," Susie said, nudging her chin and Brian's focus to the now-empty bench. "Maybe she peeks at everyone who walks by. Maybe she's too shy to start a conversation. Maybe she sits there hoping someone will engage her in conversation. Maybe she just needs a friend."

"Does that mean you think she could be the one?"

"The one?" Susie echoed. "What…"

She straightened up. Looked from Brian to the empty bench and back again. Was it possible? Was her mystery visitor the woman on the bench? Had she really been sitting just under Susie's nose the whole time?

"It could be her, you know," Brian prodded.

Was he right?

Could—

"I mean, I might've scared her away from the market, but at least until this morning when I picked you up, she had no reason to connect me to this place."

"But, assuming you're right, how would she even know where I live?" Susie asked.

"Welcome to small-town America." Brian gestured to the windshield. "Everyone knows everything about everybody."

Susie considered his words and nodded at their validity. "And it's not like I'm hard to miss. Though, how she'd known to see me as a kindred square peg before my booth officially opened is a mystery…"

"Actually, the *how* is just another reason why she might very well be the mystery visitor."

"You've lost me," Susie said, staring at Brian.

"Whoever left that message and pencil box for you prior to your first morning at the market must have read the newspaper article about you."

Susie sucked in a breath. "Yes! The newspaper article your friend did about the market! How could I have forgotten that? It came out the night before my first day. I talked about my booth's name and how my family always called me Square Peg Susie."

She shook her head. "I can't believe I didn't put that together until now. I just figured he or she saw the name of my booth and... no. They wouldn't have known to look for it if they hadn't seen it in the paper."

"And what's the woman on the bench always hiding behind?" Brian said, grinning.

Again, she looked past him to the sidewalk and the empty bench on the opposite side of the street. "A newspaper," she whispered.

Brian puffed out his chest. "I think we've solved the case of the mystery visitor. Which means now you know what to do with that money you've been putting aside in that envelope. Unless..." His chest deflated. "Unless seeing me here this morning will make her disappear again."

She sat with the possibility for a moment, weighing it from several different angles. "Assuming that doesn't happen, I think we need to handle this the way your grandmother suggested."

Brian looked a question at Susie, prompting her to continue. "Whoever left those things for me on market days wanted to remain anonymous for some reason. And when they felt that anonymity was threatened, they retreated. So, we adjust our ways and hope that makes our mystery visitor feel safe again."

"You mean like exit your place through a back door that doesn't exist for a while?"

She shook her head. "More like instead of approaching the woman on the bench with an envelope of money that may or may not be hers, I try something different."

"Such as…"

"I cast a net of kindness. That way, if it's her, maybe she'll eventually feel comfortable enough to reveal herself to me. And if it's not her, that's okay too. Because everyone needs to have a little kindness come their way now and again. Especially if they're lonely."

"A net of kindness," he repeated. "I like that."

"I do too. And it could be anything, really… Like maybe a quick wave before she hides behind her paper next time. Or, better yet, a wave and a smile." Her excitement growing, Susie leaned toward Brian, her eyes wide. "Or maybe, before she even gets there in the morning, I put a homemade cookie on the bench with a little note telling her to have a nice day. Or, since she clearly likes to read, I could leave a copy of one of my favorite books for her."

For a moment, Brian said nothing. He simply studied her, his eyes playing across her every facial feature as his own lips curved upward in a surprisingly shy smile. "Susie Walker, by any chance are you free after work tomorrow?"

Startled by both the change in subject and the expression on his face, Susie drew back. "I…I am. Yes. Why?"

"There's a concert in the park tomorrow evening, and I thought maybe we could have a picnic dinner together before it starts."

"Oh, and come up with more kindness ideas?" she asked.

"We could, sure. But…" He cleared his throat. "I was thinking mostly about just having a date with you."

"A date?" she echoed. "With me?"

"Yes, Susie. A date with you." He grabbed her hand. "So? What do you say? Would you like to have dinner with me tomorrow evening?"

"Yes. Very much, in fact."

Chapter Eleven

As per his insistence, Susie stood under the maple tree and waited while Brian readied the red and white checkered picnic blanket. All around them, couples and families were doing the same in preparation for the summer concert planned for seven o'clock, but all Susie could really think about was the man who showed with every passing moment that he'd clearly put time and thought into a date with her.

It was there in the real, honest-to-goodness picnic basket he set atop the blanket.

It was there in the plates and napkins he thought to pack.

It was there in the tantalizing aroma of the fried chicken teasing her stomach.

It was there in the chocolate chip cookies she spied just before he reclosed the basket.

And it was there in the way he looked at her as he finally beckoned her to join him.

"Welcome to our first picnic together, Susie Walker."

She sat on the blanket and looked at him across the handle of the picnic basket between them. "First?"

Brian nodded. "Of many, I hope." He waved toward the plates and the food and then returned his attention to Susie. "I hope you like chicken. It's what I picture when I think of a picnic dinner."

"Me too. And yes, I love chicken." She took the plate he held out to her and carefully filled it with the various offerings he'd arranged in containers around the outside of the wicker basket—pasta salad, grapes, strawberries, and the chicken he proudly admitted making himself. "This all looks so good. Thank you."

"Thank *you* for saying yes," he said as he too filled his plate. When they were both ready, he led them in saying grace and then settled in to eat. "Did you cast your kindness net at our mystery visitor this morning?"

She took a bite of the chicken, felt her eyes roll back in her head at its flaky goodness, and then chased it down with a sip of soda. "I did. I made a small batch of brownies, topped it with a note that wished her a happy day, and left it on my front step as I headed out."

"Was she in her usual spot?"

Nodding, Susie moved on to a bite of pasta salad. "She was. Only this time, when she sensed me looking and hid behind her newspaper, I called out that I'd left her something on my front step."

"And?"

"It was gone when I got home."

"Now, if she leaves you some sort of wooden item in the morning, we'll know she's our mystery person, right?" Brian asked.

"If she does, then yes, I guess we might."

He took a few grapes from his plate and pointed to the town's gazebo on the far side of the field. "I thought about setting us up closer to where the music will be, but then decided it might be nicer to be a little removed from the noise."

"It's a perfect spot." She redirected his attention to the walking trail on their left. "Sometimes, on my days off from the market, I like to walk here. It's very quiet and peaceful and—Ugh! Why won't they leave that poor kid alone?"

"Who?" Brian asked, looking between Susie and the trail as she rose to her feet.

"That boy, there. With the dog. Those are the same two boys who taunted him about his ears the first time I saw him."

She started toward the path only to stop as Brian caught up and put his hand on her shoulder. "Let me deal with this, Susie."

Brian hurried toward the pair of bullies. "Hey! Knock it off!"

The teens, realizing they were being addressed, froze as one, their eyes rounded in surprise. The boy they'd been mercilessly teasing whirled around, his initial surprise quickly followed by palpable relief.

"Did your parents raise you to be this way, or is this just a path you've chosen all on your own?" Brian demanded. "Either way, get out of here. And don't let me catch you bothering anyone again, got it?"

The same teen who had been so defiant with Susie opened his mouth to protest but quickly closed it when he took stock of Brian's size and demeanor. Instead, he, along with his equally mean sidekick, sprinted into the woods while Susie approached the crimson-faced dog walker.

"Are you okay?" she asked.

Dropping his gaze to the ground, the boy nodded but said nothing.

"Don't pay them any mind, okay?" Susie stopped a few feet from the boy. "People like that aren't happy. If they were, they wouldn't be so hateful."

The boy's shoulders rose and fell in what was clearly intended to be a show of indifference he couldn't quite pull off.

"Can I pet your dog?" Brian asked, pointing to the tail-wagging animal. At the boy's nod, he squatted to the ground for a nuzzle and a lick. "He's great."

"Thanks." Clearing his throat, the boy tightened his hold on the animal's leash and hiked the thumb of his free hand over his shoulder. "Anyway, I better get going. I've been gone too long as it is. But—"

"Wait. I remember you." Brian stood. "Your scout troop did a thing—a Pinewood Derby—out at my family's farm a few years ago. Jake, right? Wait, not Jake… Josh, right?"

The boy's emerald-green eyes snapped up to Brian's. "Yeah. Josh."

"Wow. You've really grown. How old are you now, Josh?"

"Fourteen."

Brian glanced at Susie. "Last time I saw this guy he was six inches shorter and—" He stopped. "Hey, how's your dad? I seem to remember him being quite a character."

"He…he's…" Josh looked at the ground again before straightening his shoulders with a resoluteness that seemed to come out of nowhere. "I gotta go."

Tugging gently on his dog's leash, Josh took a step backward toward the same offshoot path he'd taken after the first bullying session, nodded his gratitude at Brian, and then landed his eyes on Susie for the briefest of moments. "Thank you. I really wish I could look forward too."

Before she could even attempt to make sense of his words, Josh and his dog disappeared into the dusk-tinged woods with nary a trace or a sound.

"A good kid, that one," Brian said as he gently guided Susie back to their picnic blanket and the dinner they'd yet to finish. "And you say those same two boys have given him a hard time before?"

"They have."

With a gentle finger, he lifted her chin so her gaze was level with his. "Because of you, though, they stopped."

"This time, maybe. But that kind of stuff will just make him dig deeper inside himself, and he already seems like a lonely kid."

Brian sat back, handed Susie's plate to her, and popped a grape into his mouth. "From what I saw at the Pinewood Derby, he's got a great relationship with his dad. That'll keep him on track."

Oh, how she wanted to believe Brian was right. But even with the most loving, supportive parent in the world, cruelty was still cruelty, and it hurt. Deeply.

"Josh's dad was so proud that Josh had done the lion's share of the work on his derby car, unlike so many of the other kids."

Susie helped herself to a strawberry. "Meaning?"

"The building of the car for the Pinewood Derby is supposed to be a parent/son project. The parent is supposed to be there to give advice and limited assistance while the son does the majority of the work. Sadly, though, the whole competition thing tends to take over more than it should, and way too many fathers end up building the cars for their kids. But Josh and his dad didn't go that route. Josh planned, designed, cut, sanded, built, and painted his own car. And, honestly, for an eleven-year-old or whatever he was at the time, his car was incredible. He lost to some kid whose father was in construction, but everyone there knew that—based on the rules—Josh's car should've won. He clearly had a talent for woodworking and…"

His words faded against Susie's gasp as they turned, in unison, toward the spot they'd last seen the teenager—a boy who, because of a physical feature, was ridiculed by his peers and made to feel like an outsider.

"I really wish I could look forward too."

Gasping again, Susie grabbed Brian's arm. "He read the article about me," she whispered. "My quote about getting through the tough patches by looking forward… He read that, Brian."

"So maybe the woman on the bench isn't your mystery visitor at all. Maybe it's Josh."

Maybe it was…

Maybe it wasn't.

"Even if he's not, he's clearly hurting," she mused as, once again, her thoughts led her gaze to the now-empty trail. "Which means it's time for me to widen my kindness net."

Brian tossed his last grape onto his plate. "Two can cast wider than one, right?"

"Two?" Susie echoed.

"Yes. You and me. Casting that kindness net together." He smiled at her over the rim of the soda can poised in front of his lips. "What do you say?"

Grinning, she reached for her chicken leg. "I say, the more the merrier!"

Chapter Twelve

Susie swung her feet over the edge of the bed and into the bunny slippers she could just barely make out in the early dawn light peeking around her single-panel bedroom curtain. She'd tried to block out the bumps and thumps making their way through the open window beyond, but the need to know won out over the extra fifteen minutes of sleep her alarm clock would've afforded.

Yawning, she covered the limited open floor space with three steps and pushed the curtain to the side as yet another thump emanated into her room from the alley below. She looked right and saw nothing. She looked left and saw nothing. She—

Thump.

With another, bigger shove of the curtain, she pressed her head against the glass and looked straight down in time to see a piece of broken pallet sail through the air and onto a pile of similar pieces mounded on top of a rusty wagon.

Seconds later, the same stooped, white-haired man she'd spied in the same spot a few weeks earlier stepped out from behind the dumpster shared by the bookstore, the coffee house, the breakfast café, and the hardware store, grabbed the wagon's handle, and pulled it behind him until he disappeared between a gap in the hedges lining the rear of the alley.

Casting her gaze back to the dumpster, she couldn't help but feel a heaviness inside her chest. She didn't know this man who rifled through the dumpster behind her apartment, but she knew he was old. She knew he'd been there before. And she knew that no one, old or young, should have to pick through trash for things they needed. From there, her thoughts wandered to the whys and the hows and all of the other questions for which she had no answers, until she finally willed herself away from the window and into the start of a new day.

She showered, donned a green shirt, capped it off with a pair of yellow overall shorts, and added a pair of sunflower earrings to match her sunflower-adorned bobby socks. Then she pulled her hair into a high ponytail and secured it with a sunflower-adorned hair bow. She grabbed her favorite notebook and pen from her nightstand, carried it into her living room, and flopped down on her futon.

Flipping her notebook open to the list she'd started before going to bed, Susie took in the two section headings she'd made—*Bench Lady* and *Josh*—and quickly added a third: *Wagon Man*. Then, circling back to the lines beneath her first two entries, she considered the kindness ideas she'd crafted thus far.

Bench Lady:
  - *A book*
  - *A magazine*
  - *A tasty treat*
  - ~~*A hair bow*~~ *A sunflower from Brian's farm*

Josh:
  - *A new leash for his dog*
  - *Time with the farm animals?*

She thought about the elderly man she'd seen that morning and tried to imagine the kind of things that might make him happy. Maybe something edible? Maybe a kind note? Maybe fresh paint on his wagon? Maybe—

A double knock stole her attention from her list and sent it racing to her front door just as a familiar voice emerged from the other side.

"Bagel delivery for Miss Susie Walker."

Laughing, she pushed the notebook off her lap and stood, her reply beating her feet to the door. "I didn't order a bagel."

"Shh… You'll hurt its feelings."

She unlocked and opened her door, grinned at the wink she received in return, and dropped her gaze to the white paper bag Brian held in his hand. "I'm sorry, bagel. I'm very happy you're here."

"Lucky bagel." Brian held the bag out to Susie and, when she took it, gestured down the steps. "My intention was to just drop this off for you and leave you to your day off in peace. But now there's something I think you might want to see if you can spare ten, maybe fifteen minutes?"

"Sure. I have time."

"Perfect." He pointed at the bag. "Do you want to eat that here or in the truck while I drive?"

"In your truck?" she echoed. "Why? Where are we going?"

"I'd rather show you, if it's okay."

She looked between Brian and the bag and shrugged. "I can eat and go. That works."

"Then let's do it."

After handing him back the bag, she took a few moments to pop the notebook into her tote bag, grab her apartment keys, and lock up before following him and her surprise breakfast down the stairs and out onto the sidewalk.

A glance at the bench across the street as she crossed to Brian's pickup yielded the same pair of eyes that she saw peeking at her every morning as she left her apartment. Only this time, they didn't disappear behind the opened newspaper quite as quickly as usual—a triumph she pointed out to Brian the moment they were settled inside the truck together.

"Maybe the kindness net is working," Brian mused as he started the engine and stole a peek of his own.

"We can hope." Susie opened the bag Brian set on her lap and felt the answering gurgle of her stomach as the bagel came into view. "You didn't have to bring me breakfast, you know."

"It made you smile, right?"

"It did," she said. "And it still is."

"Then yes, for selfish reasons, I had to bring you breakfast."

She laughed. "Oh? And why is that?"

"My day is instantly better when it starts with a smile from you." Shifting into drive, he pulled away from the curb, his attention moving from the rearview mirror to the road ahead, to Susie, and back. "So yeah, bringing you breakfast on a day I might not normally see you just made sense."

in Peculiar, Missouri

She let go of the bag and tried to pat away the warmth borne on his words, but to no avail. "I don't know what to say to that."

"There's nothing to say. I'm just stating the facts as I've come to know them." They approached and then passed the park, stopped at the next intersection, and then turned right. "Anyway, that was my plan. Pick you up a bagel, see that smile, and then leave you to your day, as I said. But on the way here, I took some back roads I don't normally take because of some roadwork being done. And that's when I saw it."

She reached into the bag, plucked out the top half of the bagel, and stopped it just shy of her mouth. "Saw what?"

He turned right again onto a narrow, graveled lane bordering the back side of the park. Halfway down, he stopped and pointed to a well-groomed cottage beneath a canopy of oak trees. "That."

Biting a small piece from her bagel, she followed the path Brian forged with his finger, only to stop, midchew. "A birdhouse! It's another one!"

"Yup."

"Who lives here?" she demanded.

"I don't know. Mailbox just says F. Meadows. That's not a name I know from school or church or—"

Susie gasped. Pointed. "It's the same wagon! Look!"

"Wagon? What wagon?"

She tossed the top half of the bagel back into the bag. "He was in the alleyway behind my apartment just this morning, pulling wood scraps out of the dumpster. He's an elderly man. Somewhere in his early to mideighties, I think? White hair. Stooped when he walks. Fairly strong, based on the pieces of wood I see him scavenging and then pulling away in that old wagon. At the time, all I saw was that he was picking through a dumpster. And afterward, all I could think about was his age and the fact he was doing that and…"

Susie shook her head. "But he has a house. A cute one, actually. And maybe all that wood he keeps collecting has just been about building things—like that birdhouse, and the one in the park by the maintenance shed."

"And the one left in your booth along with the pencil box, the mailbox, the stick pony, the fairy house, the picture frame, and the sign for your booth," Brian added.

Taking in the house and the wagon again, Susie let herself imagine a room inside this very cottage that served as a workshop for a man clearly gifted with a talent he was reluctant for people to know about. But why? What made him a square peg? Why was he so certain people wouldn't purchase the things he made?

"It's him," she whispered. "My mystery visitor."

Brian shifted back against his seat. "It certainly looks that way. But what now? Do you want to get the money you've been setting aside for him and knock on his door?"

She thought about it for a moment. "I want to. Very much. But he stopped coming around when he thought there was a chance you might see him. Which means he isn't comfortable with us knowing who he is. I think we need to respect that. At least for now, anyway."

"But clearly he feels like an outsider in this town," Brian said. "Shouldn't we show him otherwise?"

Susie traded her view of the wagon and house for one that included the man seated beside her. There, in Brian's face, she saw a genuineness and a compassion that stole her breath and held it captive for what seemed like an eternity.

"He has talent, Susie. Real talent," Brian continued. "And I don't want the town I grew up in—or the town I want to raise my own family in one day—to be the kind of place where people feel like outsiders. It's not right. It's not what we're supposed to be about, and it's most definitely not what God would want."

Without thinking, she reached over, grabbed Brian's hand, and let the answering warmth she found there give her strength to speak. "You're a good guy, Brian Bonner. Peculiar is lucky to have you 'representing,' as they say."

"If they are, it's only because of you and how you've opened my eyes to so many things." He looked at their entwined hands and squeezed. "Not the least of which is myself and the kind of person I want to be moving forward."

"Meaning?"

"I want to see the good in everything. I want to be a light where it's needed. I want to be God's hands and feet in this world. I want to be like you, and I want to be *with*—"

A flash of movement out of the corner of her eye had her pulling her hand free and waving Brian's attention toward the elderly man emerging from behind the cottage. "That's him," she whispered. "The man I saw this morning."

They watched in silence as the elderly man disappeared inside a small shed a few yards left of the house, appeared a few minutes later with a large spool of twine, and then disappeared once again the way he'd come.

Seconds turned to minutes while they waited to see if he'd come out from behind the house again. Then, just as Susie had given up hope, he reappeared, this time with a stack of twine-wrapped wood in one hand and what appeared to be a pink scarf in his other hand. He took a few steps forward, stopped, and then looked straight at the truck.

"Uh-oh," Brian mumbled. "We're busted."

Before she could respond, the man lifted his free hand into the air and waved.

Susie waved back.

The man took a step closer. Waved again.

Susie waved a second time.

The man took another step closer. Smiled. Waved again.

This time, Brian waved too.

Another step forward, followed by a lean in their direction, had the man motioning them to come out and join him in his driveway.

"What do we do now?" Brian asked.

Grinning, Susie pushed open the passenger-side door, stepped down from the truck, and glanced back at Brian. "We accept his invitation."

Chapter Thirteen

"Good morning." Susie strode to the elderly man, her hand outstretched. "I'm Susie. Susie Walker."

"Susie," he repeated, as he set the stack of wood on the ground, covered it with the scarf, and took her hand while looking her over from head to toe. "You're even prettier than you were in that picture."

"So you know who I am?"

"I'd say it's because I'm looking at you in color as opposed to black and white, but it's more than that—something different, something special. Like it was with my Ethel." Dismissing his own words with a flick of his age-spotted hand, the man released a heavy sigh. "There I go again. Talking about things no one wants to hear. Anyway, I see you brought a friend."

Susie turned as Brian stepped up beside her and extended his hand. "I did. This is Brian."

"Bonner," Brian added. "Brian Bonner. And you are?"

The man's cheeks flushed crimson. "Seems I've gotten used to not bein' seen, doesn't it? My apologies. My name is Franklin Meadows as far as writin' checks and things. But I've always been Frank everywhere else."

He gestured to the truck parked at the end of his driveway. "So, whatcha sellin'?"

She traded glances with Brian. "We're not selling anything."

"You ain't?"

"No."

He noted the shake of Brian's head in relation to Susie's answer and drew back, surprised. "You lost then?"

"No," she and Brian said in unison.

Surprise slowly gave way to a knowing glint. "Ahhh, I see. You were lookin' for a place to neck, weren't you?"

Susie didn't need a mirror to know her face was now the red one. And she didn't need eyes on the side of her head to verify the discomfort she was all but certain Brian was feeling. Before she could recover herself enough to speak, though, Brian took the conversational baton with a surprisingly steady voice.

"I actually brought Susie here to see that." He pointed to the birdhouse.

Frank turned, nodded, and then looked back at the two of them. "It's a beaut, ain't it? Ethel would've loved it, I know." He shook his head. "And she'd be utterly ashamed of me right now for not invitin' you both in for a glass of her fresh-squeezed lemonade. Then again, I can't ever seem to make it the way she did, so I quit tryin' a long time ago. Not that I ever have any visitors, anyway."

"You don't need to invite us—"

"Enjoy your youth while you can, I say," Frank said, moving his finger back and forth between Susie and Brian. "Because before you know it, you'll be old like me. And when you are, you become invisible to people. Unless they're ahead of you going into a building or something. If they are, they might hold the door open for you, but then they roll their eyes because it's takin' you too long to walk through and you're keepin' them from gettin' wherever it is they're tryin' to go."

"Makes sense, I guess. They have places to go and things to do, and I don't. But what I don't understand is all them computers and fancy phones folks are usin' these days that make it so no one talks to each other anymore."

He dismissed his words with another wave of his hand. "Eh. I know… I know… My dinosaur is showin' again. That's why it's best I spend my days here—puttering around my garden and watching the birds who don't seem to mind that I'm old."

Propelled forward by a sadness she felt deep inside, Susie rested a gentle hand on the man's forearm. "Not everyone is too busy to listen."

"I know that now. I just needed to find a few odd ducks like myself, that's all," Frank said. "I'm the only old one in the group, but the others are all misfits in one way or another too. It's nice."

"Group?" Brian echoed.

"Technically, there's only three of us who actually show ourselves, but it's something. We meet up once a week and just talk, knowing that, at least in that moment and with each other, we fit." Tapping his chin, he eyed Susie closely. "Darla read us your reasons for movin' here, and we shared a good laugh at the notion of Peculiar bein' a place where misfits are welcome. But seein' as you've found yourself a special someone already, maybe—"

She recovered her hand to splay it between them. "Brian and I aren't boyfriend and girlfriend. We're friends."

"Then you've still fared well in a short amount of time," Frank mused. "That said, if you ever need a little lifting up, you're welcome to join us. We meet on Wednesday evenings at six thirty in the woods between here and the park. Gives us a place to belong for an hour or so."

There was so much she wanted to say, to correct, *to fix*. In the end, though, she settled on the one question that elbowed its way to the forefront of her thoughts. "Did you make that birdhouse?" she asked. "And the one just like it in the park?"

Frank's lips twitched in amusement. "Ah, I can almost hear my Ethel laughing down from heaven right now at the thought of me making something of that magnitude."

She felt the weight of Brian's disappointment mingling with her own. "So that's a no?"

"Yes," Frank said, laughing. "That's a resounding no. I was an accountant for nearly fifty years. I know math and numbers. But building things? No."

"Can we ask where you got it?" Brian asked.

"Someone left it for me underneath a tree not far from our meeting spot."

Susie leaned forward. "How do you know it was for you?"

"Because the note that was attached had my name on it." Crossing his arms, Frank rocked back on the heels of his well-worn loafers. "Told me my garden would make a nice yard for the birds."

"So whoever made it knew you liked to garden," Brian mused.

Frank nodded. "Which is why, since I have no other friends, I thought it was someone in our merry little band of misfits."

"Did you ask them?" Susie asked.

"Of course. But there's only one capable of making something like that, and he wouldn't admit to it." Frank uncrossed his arms and gestured down at the scarf-topped pile of wood scraps. "So, since someone clearly likes building things and is mighty good at it, as often as I can, I leave one of these bundles in the same spot where I found the birdhouse."

"And?" Susie asked, trading glances with Brian.

"They're always gone when I check the next morning," Frank said.

She pointed at the scarf. "And the scarf? Do you leave that too?"

"I will. But not for the same person."

"Oh?"

"I leave the wood for whoever built my birdhouse," Frank said. "The scarf is for Darla. She's a woman in our group who insists on hiding her scars in public. I know in my heart Ethel would want her to have it."

"Scars?" Susie asked.

"Bad ones," Frank said, nodding. "From a house fire."

Brian looked down at the scarf and the woodpile. "Do you ever watch to see who gets the wood?"

"No, son, that wouldn't be right." Frank pointed at the birdhouse. "I just leave them and hope someone is putting all these scraps to good use."

Susie released a slow, steady breath. "They are."

"You say that like you know," Frank said, his eyes questioning.

"Because I'm pretty sure I do." Scanning the woods bordering the rear of the elderly man's property, she thought back to the notes and items that had led her to that very spot. "In fact, I think they've been turned into a pencil box, a mailbox, a picture frame, a stick pony, another birdhouse just like yours, and a shingled sign with the name of my business carved into it."

Frank's eyebrows arched in tandem with one another. "How do you know that?"

"Because whoever made your birdhouse has been leaving me typed notes and handcrafted wooden pieces since the day I opened my booth," Susie said. "He—or she—hasn't said their name or, really, anything to help identify who they are, but I know they think they're an outsider and feel that, despite their talent, no one would be interested in buying what they make."

"Can I see them?" Frank asked.

"You mean the things they left?" At Frank's emphatic nod, she shrugged. "The shingled sign is hanging over my booth at the market as we speak, but everything else sold the moment I was given permission to do so. Which is why I was hoping, when Brian brought me to see your birdhouse, that you were my mystery visitor. So I could give you the money you've rightfully earned with your talent. But…it's not you."

"No," Frank said sadly. "It's not me."

One by one, each of them turned and looked at the birdhouse in silence, perhaps wishing, as Susie was, that it could tell them what they wanted to know. But it couldn't. Only the person who'd made it could, and he or she wasn't talking.

"How can I help them if I don't even know who they are?" she asked no one in particular.

Slowly, Frank turned, tucked an errant strand from Susie's ponytail behind her ear, and then gathered her hands inside his own. "Have faith, Susie. In the meantime, be God's light in the darkness. It'll shine the way."

"It'll shine the way…" she repeated. Rising up on her tiptoes, she planted a kiss on the elderly man's cheek. "Anyone who discounts you because of your age is a fool," she whispered.

Chapter Fourteen

They were little more than a block or two away from Main Street when Brian pulled the truck onto the shoulder and shifted into park. "I see the sun shining in the sky, and yet it's doing absolutely nothing to ward off this malaise I'm feeling right now."

"Do you think you're getting sick?" Susie swapped her view from the passenger-side window she wasn't really seeing anyway for the man looking at her from behind the steering wheel. "I could walk home from here if you want to head straight to the farm."

"No, it's nothing physical. It's…my mood, I guess. I feel it plummeting, and I think it's because of you."

She drew back. "Is it something I said? Something I did?"

"I think it's because of what you're *not* doing." He turned and faced her. "It's like the earth has slipped off its axis or something."

"I—I don't understand."

He glanced out the front windshield, shook his head, and then recaptured Susie's troubled gaze. "Ever since the moment I've met you, you've worn a perpetual smile on your face. The kind that reaches to your eyes, and your being, and everything in between. But since we left Frank's place, it's not been there—and I know, because I've looked over at you multiple times. I mean, your clothes are still happy, but *you're* not. And it feels…wrong. Really, really wrong."

"I'm sorry." She tried her best to offer the smile he sought, but, when she couldn't, she reached for the handle of her door. "I'm not meaning to be a drag on your day. I think it's best if I get out here and—"

He lunged forward across the seat, stopping her with a gentle hand from going. "No. Please. That's not what I'm saying."

"Then I still don't understand," she said, releasing the handle.

"I'm not sure how to say it right. I mean, it's everything I just said, yes, but I don't want you to leave so I can feel better. I want to help you get back to"—he spread his hands—"being *you*. The you that makes everyone's day brighter just by being near you."

It was a sweet sentiment—the kind she'd waited her whole life to hear from someone besides her mother. But the words pinged off, leaving her even sadder than she already felt.

"Talk to me, Susie. Please," Brian fairly begged. "Let me help."

Resting her cheek against the vinyl headrest, she closed her eyes, drew in a breath, and let it out in a burst of frustration. "So many people are hurting. Needlessly. Sure, things happen you can't control—sickness, the loss of a loved one, financial issues, et cetera. But the way Frank was made to feel? The way Josh is made to feel when he's trying to walk his dog? The way the woman on the bench hides herself from the world with a newspaper? It's not right, Brian."

It was as if a floodgate had opened inside her and now that she was finally talking, she couldn't stop. All the emotions she'd held back throughout so much of her own life collided with the injustices happening all around them right there in Peculiar. "Frank is old. So what? He's also experienced more in life than you or I have, or any of our peers. So why do people discount what he has to say? Why do we make people like him feel like they're no longer relevant?

"And Josh. So his ears stick out a little. Big deal. God made him that way, right? Who are we to isolate him because of it? To think it's okay to ridicule him because he doesn't look like everyone else?"

She wiped at the tears beginning to escape and willed herself to get a grip. But when she finally got herself together enough to glance back up at Brian, she was surprised to find a hint of misting in his eyes too.

"I see it too," he said, his voice thick with emotion. "Thanks to you."

"I know what it's like, always feeling different and wrong because you're not doing and being whatever it is you're supposed to do and be. But I had my mom in my corner every step of the way, reminding me that I was God's child and that I mattered." She blew out another breath. "It just makes me sad people can be so cruel to one another about such unimportant things. I mean, so I wear weird stuff and get excited about things people think are silly. Who does that hurt? I'm still a person."

"An amazing person," Brian added.

"And Frank can't walk terribly fast anymore and doesn't understand technology. Who does that hurt? He's a sweet man who worries about people and wants to do what he can to help them. What's so unappealing about that that we, as a society, shut him out of conversations and make him feel as if he's suddenly invisible?"

Brian shook his head. "I don't know, Susie. But one thing I do know is that you made him smile, just like you make me and everyone else at the market smile."

"Big deal," she murmured.

With the pad of his thumb, he wiped away a tear making its way down her cheek and then tilted her chin up until she had nowhere to look but at him. "It *is* a big deal, Susie. Don't discount that. Ever."

"A smile?" She grimaced. "Please. What does that do?"

"It changes people, Susie."

"Who? When?"

"The other vendors at the market, for starters," Brian said. "Before you, the vibe there was different. People came in the morning, sold their stuff, and beat it out of there when they were done. Everyone saw themselves as their own little entity, completely separate from everyone else. But since you, it's been different. I see people interacting in ways they didn't before. And I hear them pointing customers to each other's booths."

"You don't know that's because of me," Susie protested.

"Yeah, I do. I saw it with Frank just now too. The man who stepped out from behind that house while we were in the truck was a very different man by the time we left. He walked lighter. He smiled. The difference was undeniable."

She waved at his words. "I think you're seeing things that aren't there."

"You could make a case for that, I suppose, if my examples were all based on observation, but one isn't. That one is based on personal experience."

"Meaning?"

"The way you are? Your smile? The way you care about people? It's changing me, Susie. Into a person who sees beyond my own little world in ways I'm ashamed to say I don't think I ever really did before." He stopped and took a breath. "I'm lying awake at night now thinking about places I can spread kindness—things I can do to help get this town back to what it was for Nana yet clearly isn't for people like Josh and Frank."

"You are?" she managed to eke out past the lump forming in her throat.

"I am. And that's because of you, Susie. You walk the walk. You don't just talk about kindness. You spread it. You don't just talk about God. You embrace Him. You lead by example regardless of who is or isn't paying attention."

"I don't know what to say."

"You don't have to. You just have to know how special you are."

For several long moments, she simply sat there, unable to catch her breath in relation to the things he'd said about her—things she'd never heard from anyone outside her family before. It was a lot to take in, a lot to process. Eventually, though, she leaned over, plucked her notebook from her tote bag, and handed it to Brian.

"What's this?" he asked.

"I've been working on a list of kindnesses. Last night, I wrote some for the lady on the bench, and for Josh. And, before you came by this morning, I was starting to think about what I could do for the man by the dumpster—Frank."

Brian tapped the top of the notebook. "So can I look?"

"Of course."

She watched as he opened the book, flipped through to the page she'd paperclipped the previous night, and began to read. When he reached the bottom of the list, he looked back up at Susie. "I like the idea of getting Josh out to see the farm animals."

"Me too." She pointed at the empty space at the bottom of the page. "And maybe I could pick up a fresh can of paint for Frank's wagon… Think he'd like that?"

Brian shook his head before she'd even finished. "I don't know, Susie. The wagon I saw just now needs a lot more than a new paint job. At least two of the wheels looked like they were barely hanging on. And the rust? There was way too much to even think about painting over."

"Rats." She took the notebook back from him and stared down at the lines she hoped to fill for their new friend. "Maybe some seed packets for his garden? Or a watering can I can decorate? Or maybe offer to drive him and his scraps to his place if I happen to be home the next time he comes—"

Sliding back into place behind the steering wheel, Brian shifted the pickup into drive, his attention bouncing between Susie and his sideview mirror. "Actually, if it's okay, can I drop you off at your place? I have an errand I'd like to run."

***

She was rinsing out her paintbrushes when she heard the knock. Setting them on the dish towel she'd placed beside the sink, she shut off the water and hurried to open the door.

"You're back."

"I'm back." Looking past her, he grinned at the medley of items strewn across her tablecloth-topped floor. "It looks like you've been busy while I was gone."

Gesturing him inside, she led the way into her sun-drenched living room. "For Josh, I found a dog dish at the hardware store and decided to paint it." She picked up the bowl and slowly turned it around for Brian to see.

in Peculiar, Missouri

"A bone… A ball… A"—his eyes widened on hers—"cat?"

She looked at him sheepishly over the rim of the bowl. "Uh-oh. It looks more like a mouse, doesn't it?"

"No, no, it's a cat—a real good one, in fact. Very detailed. But on a dog's bowl?"

"Is there some rulebook somewhere that says dogs must hate cats?" she asked.

Brian laughed. "No, but that's usually the way it works."

"Hmm. Maybe I should change it to a dog?" she asked, eyeing her creation. "I think I can."

He took the bowl out of her hands and held it over her head. "No. You'll leave it just like this. It's fine."

"You really think so?"

"I do." He handed her the bowl and pointed at the picture of a sunflower. "Did you paint that in the time I've been gone?"

She nodded. "I mean, we can still give the woman on the bench a sunflower from your farm, but this one won't die."

"Good thinking."

Setting the bowl back down, she pointed at her notebook. "So now I have something for Josh and the woman on the bench. I tried to find a watering can I could paint for Frank when I bought the bowl, but they didn't have any good ones."

"That's okay," Brian said. "Because I have something for him out in my truck."

"In your truck?" she echoed.

"C'mon… Come see."

Taking the hand he offered, she followed him down the steps, onto the sidewalk, and over to the edge of the curb where his pickup was parked. There, carefully strapped into the truck bed, was a shiny new oversized red wagon with an equally shiny red bow affixed to the handle.

"You—you bought Frank a new wagon?" she stammered.

"I did." His right hand still in hers, he reached into the truck with his left. "I'm telling you, Susie, the one he's got now isn't long for this world. Maybe one or two more trips to town if he's lucky. But this"—he ran his fingers along the edge of the wagon—"should last him a long time."

Stepping forward, she pulled Brian in for a hug she felt clear down to her toes. "You're a good man, Brian Bonner," she whispered. "A very, very good man."

Chapter Fifteen

She was just feeding a new piece of paper into the typewriter when Brian stepped into her booth and peeked over her shoulder.

"I've been riding high all day on the image of Frank opening his front door this morning and finding his brand-new wagon. Yet, right now, in this moment, I'm back to feeling like a complete louse watching you load that thing up on the off chance your mystery visitor will finally return."

"Don't. Please." Susie turned around, plucked a piece of lint off Brian's shirt, and then made her way over to the table for her tote bag. "Square Peg Susie's had another successful day."

Brian took in the half-empty shelves lining her booth. "I can see that."

"Even the bows are starting to take off."

"I told you. With you as a model, how could they not?"

"Ha!" She slid her bag onto her shoulder and pointed toward the exit. "Ready to head out?"

"Why do you do that?" he asked, following her down the main aisle.

She stopped, midstep, to stare up at him. "Do what?"

"Assume that a compliment paid to you is a joke."

"Because they always are. I mean, look at me." She spread her arms and then continued walking toward the day's lowering sun just beyond the market's outer wall. "I'm not exactly something you'd see in a clothing catalog or fashion magazine."

Brian quickened his pace in order to keep up. "Pity. For the catalog and the consumer."

"Ha—"

Placing a hand on her shoulder, Brian gently spun her around. "Stop. I'm not joking."

"C'mon, Brian. I get that you're a nice guy. That you've taken the time to see beyond my exterior—for which I'm grateful, by the way. But I've been on the receiving end of double, triple, and quadruple takes since I've been old enough to dress myself. I've heard it all. Banana Girl… Can you tweet, Canary Girl?… Yellow submarine… And that's just when I wear yellow. Other choices earn other names. But you get the idea."

"I do. But *I* don't think that, and *I* don't see that," Brian protested.

She began walking again. "Then you probably have tritanopia. That not only makes it so you can't tell the difference between yellow and pink, for example, it also makes colors look less bright."

"Oh for Pete's sake," he mumbled.

"Seriously, Brian. It's a thing."

He shook his head, followed her out to the spot on the sidewalk where they normally turned right, and stopped. "Unfortunately, while I'd love to stay and argue with you, I can't walk home with you or sit in the park hoping to see Josh like we talked about. I want to, very much, but when I saw Nana on my way into the market this morning, she mentioned a list of things that need doing in and around her place. I promised to do them after work if she'd just wait.

She agreed, but I know if I take too long getting out there, she'll find her way up a ladder she has no business climbing at her age."

She fought against the instinct to slump and, instead, shooed him in the direction of his truck. "Go. Please. I've always thought it was silly that you walk me into town only to turn around and walk back to your truck."

"There's a book I've been meaning to get," he said, grinning. "I just keep forgetting, is all."

Susie rolled her eyes, laughing as she did. "Go help your grandmother, and I'll see you on Thursday."

His smile disappeared. "Thursday? But that's two days away."

"I know. Market days are Tuesdays, Thursdays, and Saturday."

"So…"

She stared at him. "So, the next one is Thursday."

"Right. But we have things to do—kindnesses to spread, remember?" At her nod, he took a halfhearted step in the direction of his truck. "Which means we have work to do. Which, in turn, means I'll see you tomorrow."

"Okay."

"Okay?" he repeated.

"Okay." She started toward town, stopped, then looked back to find him watching her. "Your grandmother? A ladder?"

"I'm going."

And sure enough, he went, leaving her to head to town on her own. Along the way, she took notice of a few birds, a passing dog with its owner, and even a new patch of wildflowers springing up on the eastern edge of the park, but it was different than it was when Brian was there to see it with her. It was an unfamiliar if not downright unsettling feeling, and she did her best to shove it aside in favor of searching for Josh.

She walked in the area of the gazebo…nothing.

She looped around the children's play area…nothing.

She wandered by the dog park…nothing.

No sign of Josh. No sign of his dog.

On her second pass by the gazebo, she spotted the same two teenage boys who seemed to take such joy in bullying Josh. But, still, no sign of Josh.

Doubling back toward the path that meandered along the edge of the woods, she kept walking until she came to the same unpaved trail she'd seen Josh and his dog take in the past. A glance at her watch and then the sky gave her pause, but, in the end, curiosity won out and she veered onto the path.

A few feet in, she spotted a small white placard affixed to a tree and realized she was on a marked trail that wound through the woods, over a narrow bridge spanning a small pond, and dumped her in front of a large tree denoting the start of two new trails. The red trail would take her to the left. The green trail to the right. She opted for green only to come across another choice less than a hundred feet later. This time, she went left on yellow, only to veer off course completely when she noticed a break in the trees.

She stepped through the opening and drew to a stop at the sight of five stumps arranged in a circle like chairs around a firepit. Grateful for a chance to tighten the laces on her sneakers, she wandered over to the first stump and sat down. While she tied, she looked around, taking in the thick trees, the feeling of being tucked away from the rest of the—

She straightened up and looked at the other stumps.

"This is it," she murmured. "The place where Frank and his friends meet."

She rose and wandered from stump to stump, imagining the elderly man and his friends sitting in that very spot, desperately holding on to the feeling of being part of something. Of mattering. Of being heard. Of being seen. It was something she would've loved when she lived in Connecticut yet no longer needed now that she was in Peculiar.

Yet Frank was in Peculiar.

And the people he met in that very spot each week were in Peculiar.

She breathed through the urge to cry and, instead, made her way back through the gap in the trees and onto the path, picking her way around sticks and rocks as she went. Another fifty yards or so down the path she caught a glimpse of a tired, run-down wall perched on a hill off to her left. A second, more thorough look yielded not only a single wall but an entire cottage that looked as if a good swift wind could reduce it to rubble. Everything about the building suggested it had been long abandoned except the heavy curtains that covered the windows—

Snap!

Susie whirled toward the path, her eyes skittering in the direction she'd just come.

"Hello?" she called.

No answer.

No sound.

She waited another minute, her ears on high alert, but when there was still nothing, she turned to the house, her eyes narrowing in on the home's lone open window and the curtain she'd sworn had—

Snap!

Jerking her head to the trail, Susie surveyed her surroundings, relief loosening the knot of fear in her shoulders as a squirrel scurried off in the opposite direction. She started to turn back to the house a third time but stopped as her gaze fell on another barely discernible gap in the trees. Curious, she peeked through the opening and spied the exact same clearing as before, only this time she was seeing it from the north side rather than the south.

Once again, she stepped into the clearing and over to the stumps, her eyes moving slowly around the wall of trees. A flash of movement on her second pass yielded a dog's nose doing its due diligence beneath a wild azalea bush. A more extensive look showed that the dog was on a leash.

"Hello?" she called. "Who's there?"

The dog looked at something behind it and then turned back to Susie, its tongue appearing and disappearing between pants and swallows. Ducking down, she gazed past the dog to the familiar face peeking at her from behind a tree.

"Josh?"

The face disappeared, but the dog remained in place, letting her know the boy was still there, within hearing range.

"My name is Susie," she said. "We've seen each other twice now in the park. And the second time I saw you, I was with my friend,

in Peculiar, Missouri

Brian. You had your Pinewood Derby at his farm when you were younger. He said the car you built was amazing."

When there was still no movement beyond the dog's, she slid her tote bag off her arm and onto the ground. "I made you something," she said. "For your dog."

She unzipped her bag, reached inside, and pulled out the silver bowl. "I wanted to put her name on it, but since I didn't know it, I went with some little pictures instead. Brian reminded me that dogs don't like cats, so maybe that one isn't so good."

"Lindy—*sniff*—doesn't mind cats."

"Okay, good." She sat down on a stump with the bowl in her lap. "If you want, I could still add Lindy along the bottom edge. It would fit real nice."

"Why'd you make a bowl for my dog?"

"Because I was thinking about you and thought that might be a nice thing to do."

A series of sniffles was soon followed by the emergence of first the dog and then Josh into the clearing. Even in the dusky light, she could tell he'd been crying.

"Did they bother you again?" she asked, rising to her feet.

Josh stole a glance in her direction and then looked away. "Who?"

"Those boys from the park."

For a moment, it looked as if Josh was going to laugh. Instead, he wiped his face with the back of his free hand and shook his head.

"Have you been making things out of wood and leaving them for me at the market?" she asked, surprising even herself with the question.

His answering laugh held no shred of humor. "Making things?" he echoed.

"Yes. Like a birdhouse that looks like a Victorian house, and—"

"Frank already asked me if I made that, and I told him I didn't."

"Wait." She stared at him. "Frank? As in Frank Meadows?"

"I don't know, maybe." Josh took another swipe at his face. "He's old like a grandpa, and his hair is white."

"Is he a friend of your dad's? she asked.

"No. I just...know him, that's all."

She tucked the information aside for further processing at a later time and swung the conversation back to her original question. "So you didn't make that birdhouse or any other birdhouse like it? You didn't make a pencil box or a stick pony or a mailbox or a picture frame or a sign either?"

"Nope." Josh shifted his dog's leash to his opposite hand. "Why would you think I did?"

"Because Brian said you showed real talent for woodworking when you made that car with your scout troop a few years back, and I thought maybe...because of those boys...you were feeling like a square—" She stopped and held the freshly decorated dog bowl out to him. "Anyway, this is for Lindy."

Josh took the bowl, looked at it, and then squatted down to show it to his dog. When it passed the smell test, Josh settled his unseeing gaze just left of Susie. "I *wish* I'd made that stuff. I liked working with wood when I was younger—or maybe I liked it because it was another thing I could do with my dad.

"He's my best friend, you know? He taught me how to fish, how to swim, how to climb a tree, how to think through building that derby car, and just about everything else I know. Doing things with him made it so it didn't matter that he was my only friend. Because we did real stuff together."

"Sounds like you and your dad have a great relationship," she mused.

"We do." Josh swallowed. Hard. "Did."

A sense of dread ballooned inside her chest—a dread she hoped and prayed was unfounded. "Did your dad die?"

"He almost did. A few weeks ago. But the doctor says he'll be okay. In time."

"Oh, thank God."

Josh toed a stone back and forth in front of him. "He's in a place now, down in Kansas City, trying to build up his strength again. Which means, because of school, I only get to see him on the weekends, and only if my mom isn't working and can take me. In the meantime, now that Dad is on the mend, she wants me to concentrate on finally"—he lifted his fingers to simulate quote marks—"making friends my own age at school."

"And you don't want to do that?" Susie asked.

"Have you not seen *these*?" Josh pointed at his ears. "Because everyone in school sure does. And if they don't care at first, that changes real quick thanks to Liam and Hudson."

"I take it those are the boys in the park?"

Tightening his mouth, Josh kicked the stone and then blindly wiped at a tear he clearly didn't want Susie to see. "In the park… At school… On the bus… Everywhere."

"Does your mother know about them?" she asked.

"No. And I don't want her to. Ever." He wiped at his face again. "She's just now starting to smile again."

Susie lowered herself back onto a stump, her thoughts racing. "I could talk to your principal and ask him to—"

"No. Please." Josh tugged his dog closer and led her over to the second gap Susie had discovered. "I don't need school friends. I just need my dad to hurry up and get well so he can come home again."

Then, raising the bowl up a few inches, he nodded at Susie. "Lindy and I thank you for this."

Chapter Sixteen

Step by step, they maneuvered their way through a labyrinth that looked very different in the limited moonlight playing peekaboo between the trees. When there were more gaps in the canopy above, they could pick out exposed roots and the occasional rock that might otherwise be a tripping hazard. Where the canopy was lush, they relied on the cell phone Brian hadn't realized was running low on battery.

"It should be just around this next bend." Susie stopped, waited for Brian to catch up, and then led the way around a fallen oak tree marking the next choice in trails. "This is where I'm pretty sure I went left."

Brian shone his light at the pair of triangle markers affixed to the tree's trunk, and laughed. "Considering the trail on the left is yellow, I see no reason to doubt you."

"Smart man."

Shifting the ever-dimming beam to the left, Brian helped Susie over a gnarled root only to groan as they were plunged into darkness. "A smart man would've checked his cell phone *before* going into the woods at night."

"You didn't know we were going, remember?"

"True." He stopped them in the middle of the trail. "Let's just stand here for a second. Let our eyes adjust to—

"Shh…"

"What do you hear?" Brian whispered.

"Voices," she whispered back.

"I don't hear…" Brian's words faded into nothing as he took her hand and carefully walked her forward. "There's some sort of light coming from beyond those trees."

Sure enough, as they moved forward toward the light, the voices grew silent.

She tried to make out the first of the two gaps in the trees that would deliver them into the clearing, but when she couldn't, she turned her head in the direction she knew it to be. "Frank? It's Susie and Brian. From the other day."

A beat of silence on the other side of the trees gave way to first a light drawing closer, and next, Frank's smiling face peeking at them through the now visible gap. "You came," he said, motioning them forward.

Together, Brian and Susie made their way through the gap and into the same clearing she'd found the previous day. Only this time, instead of five empty stumps, the light from Frank's lantern showed only three were unoccupied. The fourth held a figure she couldn't make out in the dark, and the fifth housed one she'd hoped she'd see.

"I hope it's okay that we're here," Susie said, swinging her attention back to the elderly man.

"Of course it's okay. Come… Come… Sit." Frank shone the light on the empty stumps until Brian and Susie were both seated and then set the lantern down in the center of the circle. "We've been encouraging Josh to use his interests to meet people—people who will appreciate him for the smart, caring, thoughtful young man he is."

"That's good advice," Susie said.

"You like animals, right, Josh?"

Susie looked over the light to the other side of the circle to see who was speaking, but the shadows were too thick to see much of anything.

"Yeah, because animals don't care if I have big ears," Josh said. "They see only the stuff that matters."

"The right people will see the same thing," the woman said. "Just keep trying."

The boy's shoulders lifted with a shrug Susie could barely make out in the low light. "Shouldn't you take your own advice, Darla?"

"It's different for me, Josh."

"How?" Frank and Josh asked in unison.

"People turn away when they see me."

Frank smacked his leg. "Then they're fools."

"So are all the people who see only an old man when they look at you," Josh murmured. "Because they're missing out."

On and on the conversation went while Susie listened, the love the unlikely trio had for each other every bit as tangible as the stumps and the lantern that defined the very place they came to feel safe. To connect. To matter. A peek at Brian showed that he too was moved by the conversation taking place around them.

"I would've loved to have had a group like this when I was growing up in Connecticut," Susie said during a lull in the conversation. "Maybe I would've felt less alone, less...I don't know."

"Less like a square peg?" Darla interjected from across the clearing.

Susie jerked her gaze to Brian. "Wait. Are-are you the one? The one who was leaving me those notes on my typewriter? The one who made all of those beautiful handcrafted wooden pieces?"

She rocketed up onto her feet. "Because if you are, I have the money you've made from—"

"I can't make anything," Darla said.

"But—"

Frank set his hand on Susie's arm. "Darla's face and hands were severely burned in a house fire a few years ago. That's why she wears a scarf and gloves."

"A scarf and gloves?" Susie echoed as, once again, she looked at Brian for confirmation she'd heard correctly.

Brian, in turn, leaned forward, his voice gentle and kind. "You're the woman who sits on the bench across from Susie's place…"

"I am." The woman shifted just enough to afford Susie a quick view of the pink scarf that had belonged to Frank's late wife, Ethel, and the same black gloves she'd been seeing for weeks now.

"But why?" Susie asked.

"Your spirit leapt off the page when I read about you in the paper. It made me happy. Then, when I saw you in person, everything about you—your clothes, your joy, your smile, the bounce in your step as you walk into each new day—made me happy. Soon, seeing that every morning became the one bright spot in my day."

She felt Brian's eyes on her but couldn't make herself meet them. "Then if it's not you, and it's not Frank, and it's not Josh, who is it? Who makes these things? Who else in this town feels like we do, like they don't truly—

A faint light just beyond the clearing caught her up short. "Is that light coming from that old house over there?" she asked, pointing toward the far end of the clearing.

"What house?" Brian asked, his brow furrowing.

"It's just this old, run-down place on the other side of those trees." Again, she looked toward the faint pinpoint of light. "The place looks abandoned, but I'm pretty sure someone watched me from one of the windows yesterday."

"That's the hermit," Josh said as Frank nodded his agreement.

"You mean Old Man Rogers?" Brian stood, walked toward the light, and peeked between the gap. "Yup, that's his place."

"He's a silent member of our group."

Susie turned and stared at Frank. "Silent member?"

"We think he listens in on our meetings."

"Why do you think that?" Brian asked.

"Because we hear him open his window as we're getting started and then close it when we're leaving." Frank tapped his chin. "It's the only thing that makes sense with...you know."

"What?" Susie prodded.

"I share with the group how much I like birds...and a birdhouse is left here. Darla talks about wanting to cover the scars on her face with pretty scarves...and a packet of scarves is left here. Josh—"

Susie held up her hand. "But *you* gave her the pink scarf."

"Spurred on by how happy the others made her," Frank said.

Susie took it all in. "And for Josh?"

"A journal was left for me when it looked like my dad was going to die," Josh said.

She looked around the circle. "And it wasn't one of you doing it for the others?"

All three heads shook in unison.

"I guess he sees you all as kindred spirits—people who understand what it is to be overlooked or cast aside," she hypothesized aloud. "But this is the first meeting I've been to. How could he have known about me?"

Darla cleared her throat and shifted on her stump. "Every week, when I finish reading the paper, I leave it on his front porch. So he'll feel less disconnected from the world."

He'd read about her in the paper...

He'd connected with her over being a square peg...

He'd had easy access to needed materials thanks to Frank...

It all made perfect sense.

Except for one thing.

"In order to type those notes and leave those things in my booth, he had to have left his house," Susie murmured. "Would a hermit do that?"

"In the middle of the night? In a town like Peculiar?" Brian blew out a long, labored breath. "Maybe. Unless or until some idiot camped out in a car and made him feel unsafe to leave his house."

She considered the possibility as she looked around the circle, drinking in each and every person present.

At Frank, who felt as if he was no longer relevant in a world that gave him little reason to believe otherwise.

At Josh, who was ridiculed because of a feature God gave him.

And, finally, at Darla, a woman who felt more comfortable hiding in the shadows—convinced that no one would ever see past the scars on her face and hands to the person she still was deep inside.

"We have to do better," Susie said, standing again. "We just have to."

Chapter Seventeen

A Month Later

Susie looked across the rim of her lemonade glass at Rhoda and silently noted the curve of the woman's jaw, the shape of her slender nose, and the way her smile sparkled in her eyes the same way her grandson's smile did.

"Would you mind if I added a fairy to the mural outside my front door and made her look just like you?" Susie asked.

Rhoda leaned back in her rocking chair. "Fairies are supposed to be little bitty things, aren't they?"

"Not in my mural they aren't."

"Then, to answer your question, I'd be honored. Thank you, Susie."

Susie ran her fingers across the baby chicks adorning her yellow dress and then looked out over the part of Grey-Oaks Farm she could see from Rhoda's front porch. "How's Josh working out with the animals?"

"He's working out just fine. The goats come running the second he steps off that school bus on Thursday afternoons." Rhoda tsked softly. "I tell them not to get too used to him, though."

She abandoned her view of the farm in favor of Brian's grandmother once again. "Why?"

She chuckled. "Because that boy hasn't noticed the girl who sits behind him on the bus quite yet. But she's sure noticed *him*."

"Why do you say that?" Susie asked, toeing her rocker to a stop.

"I've been around a long time, my dear, and I know puppy-dog eyes when I see them."

"Should I tell him the next time I see him?"

Rhoda, too, stopped rocking. "No, he'll figure it out. When it's time. For now, let's let him enjoy his time with his animal friends."

Susie smiled—a smile that grew still wider at the sound of a truck door closing in the distance. "Sounds like Brian is back."

"Indeed it does." Rhoda shifted forward in her chair just enough to see around the corner of her porch and then lifted her hand in a wave. "Good afternoon, Frank."

"I brought Scrabble, a record with that song you asked about the other day, and some pictures of Ethel and me I thought you might—" Frank stopped just shy of the porch step. "Susie, hello. I didn't know you were here. Want to play Scrabble with two oldsters like Rhoda and me?"

Brian, who lagged behind, quickened his pace over to the porch. "Actually, if she doesn't mind, I'd like to steal Susie away for a little while first." He slanted a sheepish glance Susie's way. "Is that okay?"

"Of course." She pushed off the rocker, planted a kiss on first Rhoda's cheek and then Frank's as she passed him on the steps to meet up with Brian. "What's up?"

"Walk with me?" he asked, pointing to the barn.

"Sure. Is everything okay?"

"Why don't you ask me that again in about ten minutes? I'll be able to answer then."

A trio of goats grazing on the edge of the driveway lifted their heads as her laugh rang through the air. "Sounds mysterious, but okay…"

Together, they followed Rhoda's flagstone walkway around the corner of her house to the fence that ran the length of the strawberry field. She waited for him to speak, but when he didn't, she went ahead and filled the void with the news she'd been waiting to share with him since she'd arrived at the farm.

"He thanked me for the money," she said.

Brian stopped, midstep, to stare down at Susie. "Old Man Rogers? He spoke to you?"

"His name is actually Joe. And no, he typed it."

"He came back to the market?" he asked.

She grinned. "Nope. Darla suggested I take the typewriter to him, and I did. Left it right there on his front porch with the envelope of money sitting on top."

"Wow. Nice job."

"Thank you." She did a little jig right there in front of him, her rain boots tapping on the dry earth. "So, what did you want to talk to me about?"

He wandered over to the fence, ran his finger along the top edge, and then turned around and reached for her hand. "I've been thinking."

"Uh-oh," she teased.

"I've been thinking about the whole square-peg thing."

She stared up at him. "And…"

"I don't think life is supposed to be like that. I think there's room for everyone. You've shown me that these last few months." He laced his fingers with hers and pulled her close. "And now I'm hoping that maybe you'll consider making room for me. In your life."

She frowned. "You're already in my life, silly."

He looked up at the sky, shook his head, and mumbled something unintelligible. Then he lowered his gaze back to Susie's. "Focus for a minute, okay?"

"I'm focused."

"I'm hoping you'll consider making room for me in your life as your boyfriend."

"My boyfriend?" she echoed.

"Yes."

"You mean you want *me* to be *your* girlfriend?"

He looked left. He looked right. He looked behind him. "Do you see anyone else standing here?"

"No."

"Then yeah, I'm asking you."

"But I'm—"

"Perfect for me," he said.

She looked down at her boots and her dress and then back up at Brian and the smile that melted her heart and made it so there was only one answer she could give. "I would love for you to be my boyfriend."

This time, when she did a jig, Brian joined in, his arms and feet moving every bit as fast as Susie's. When they finished, she stepped forward into his waiting arms.

"Okay, you can ask me again now," he said between kisses.

"Ask you what?"

"Your question from before."

in Peculiar, Missouri

"My question from before… My question from before…" She thought back until she hit on the question he was referring to. "Oh, right! Yes! I've got it now."

His smile sparkled his eyes. "Go ahead. I'm waiting."

"Is everything okay?" she asked.

"Actually, yes. Everything is *incredible*."

Dear Reader,

First off, thank you for reading our "Peculiar" stories. When Laura and I sat down to pick a town, we loved the idea of playing with who would live in a town named Peculiar. It was a bonus to find that the town's website has a letter from 1899 from the postmaster of the day, explaining the origins of the name.

Readers always ask where a story comes from. I like to say writers are like magpies—we pick up bright and shiny bits from here and there. I grew up in the country on a farm much like the ones in Rhoda's 1960 story. We lived outside the town and, of course, there was an annual festival. And as an introvert, I've always felt a little peculiar myself. Writing Rhoda's story and exploring her feelings of being a tall woman who was more comfortable with plants than people, I could relate with her insecurities.

The history of our towns, the history of our lives, gives us a connection to the land and to those who came before. Writing these stories gave us the blessing to create a home for our characters. A place where we all can fit in, no matter how we feel about our place in the world.

Welcome home,
Emily Quinn and Laura Bradford

About the Authors

Emily Quinn

Emily Quinn loves hanging out in her Tennessee home watching for deer and cooking new recipes when she's not thinking of stories to keep her busy on the keyboard. She shares her cabin in the woods with her husband and two Keeshonds who think they rule the house, if not the world.

Laura Bradford

While spending a rainy afternoon at a friend's house as a child, Laura Bradford fell in love with writing over a stack of blank paper, a box of crayons, and a freshly sharpened number-two pencil. From that moment forward, she never wanted to do or be anything else.

When she's not writing, Laura loves to bake, travel, and advocate for those living with multiple sclerosis.

Story Behind the Name

Peculiar, Missouri

The town began with a plat map completed and filed on July 29, 1868, by Robert Cass as "The Town Of Peculiar." The name came from the postmaster, E.T. Thompson. Mr. Thompson's first choice for the town name was Excelsior. Unfortunately, that name and the three other names Mr. Thompson sent into the post office officials had already been claimed in Missouri. Frustrated, he told the officials to just give them a name but said "it would not do to give us some 'peculiar' name."

The powers that be either misunderstood Mr. Thompson's plea or they were tired of his letters. And so Peculiar, Missouri, was born.

Peculiar is near the Kansas/Missouri border in Cass County and is four square miles with a current population of 2600. That number grows to 7500 when you include the surrounding farms. The perfect small town for a cozy and inclusive mystery!

Apple Crumb Bread

Ingredients:

½ cup butter
1 cup sugar
2 eggs
1 teaspoon baking soda in
    2 Tablespoons milk

2 cups flour
½ teaspoon salt
1 teaspoon vanilla
1½ cups chopped and peeled
    apples

For topping:

1 teaspoon cinnamon
2 Tablespoons butter

4 Tablespoons flour
2 Tablespoons brown sugar

Directions:

Preheat oven to 325 degrees.

    Cream together in a bowl, the butter, sugar, and eggs. Add the baking soda dissolved in milk. Then add the flour, salt, vanilla, and apples.

    Pour into a 9×5½-inch greased bread pan. Sprinkle with the topping mixture (can be difficult to "sprinkle"—just do your best).

    Bake for 1 hour, until toothpick comes out clean. Cool on wire rack and share with a new friend!

Read on for a sneak peek of another exciting book in the Love's a Mystery series!

Love's a Mystery *in* Crooksville, Ohio
by Johnnie Alexander & Dana Lynna

The Potter's Design

By Johnnie Alexander

Crooksville, Ohio
Summer 1938

Jasper Kane stood beneath the hickory tree and stared at the sign above the two-story structure with the same unsettling mixture of pride and guilt he'd felt every day since the funeral.

KANE POTTERY

OUT OF FIRE COMES STRENGTH.

The manufacturing company wasn't the biggest in the region, appropriately christened the Pottery Capital of the World, nor was it the most innovative or competitive. But its founding focus on manufacturing utilitarian pottery—dishes, serving bowls, pitchers—for utilitarian purposes at a utilitarian price had kept the pottery wheels turning and the kilns burning throughout the worst years of the Great Depression. Not a single employee had been let go, an accomplishment old Edmund Kane attributed solely to his superior business acumen.

Perhaps he'd been right. But Edmund now rested in Crooksville Memorial Cemetery, and the mantle of responsibility now rested on Jasper.

Who hoped to implement the product line his father had forbidden.

In what had become a morning ritual, Jasper took a deep breath, adjusted his hat, and strode toward the concrete steps leading to the brick building's thick wooden doors. Once inside, he greeted everyone he met on his way to the mezzanine office with the half wall of glass that overlooked the warehouse floor.

He paused outside the door and placed one hand on the frosted glass pane that bore his name and shut his eyes. When he opened them again, his name was still on the door. Rightfully so—this was his office now.

Yet it didn't seem right. Until only a few weeks ago, the name Edmund Kane had been imprinted in big block letters as a subtle means of intimidation for all those who entered the Boss's private domain. Jasper went with a smaller, friendlier font as a subtle message that he wasn't his dad and his door was open to anyone.

Especially anyone with new ideas for a shift from the utilitarian mundane to more artistic products.

He entered the office, still feeling like an interloper, and set his briefcase on the broad desk. His suit jacket went on the coat hook behind the door, then he rolled up the sleeves of his white dress shirt. Time to work. Time to plan. Time to call Vernon Spears.

During a long and sleepless night, Jasper had tossed and turned, pondered and prayed, and finally risen before sunrise with a pathetic plan.

He wanted to give Vernon the benefit of the doubt, to believe that the owner of Spears Ceramics would have a logical explanation for his latest venture. But the knot in Jasper's stomach told him those hopes were as fragile as the most delicate porcelain.

The direct approach—one he didn't want to take—was the only way to find out for sure.

Almost as soon as the operator connected the call, Vernon's baritone voice roared through the line loudly enough that Jasper held the receiver a few inches from his ear.

"What can I do for you, Jasper? Need my advice now that your daddy's gone? I'm telling you again, son, you should think about liquidating. Best thing for you to do. I'll make you a fair offer on your equipment and your inventory. Then you can put that building to a more profitable use."

Jasper envisioned the older man, sweat glistening on his bald pate, thick fingers gripping the phone, feet propped on his desk as he leaned back in his chair.

"Thank you for your concern, Mr. Spears, but I have no plans to close these doors," Jasper replied. "There's only one thing bothering me right now."

"What would that be, son?"

Jasper pulled the pamphlet from his briefcase and opened it. "This new line of decorative ceramics you're advertising to your retailers. You're calling it 'Autumn Decor.'"

"Aw, yes. The ladies in this fair land have denied themselves too long, if you ask me. They want something new and pretty to put on their mantels. As proof to their neighbors that they've got more than two dimes in their change purses again. You know how it is." Vernon's voice didn't reveal even the slightest tremor. The man had no shame. "What do you think of our new pieces?"

"Those are my designs." Unfortunately, Jasper's voice did waver. He closed his eyes and inhaled a silent breath. He dared not sound weak. He firmly enunciated each word. "You have no right to them."

"Well now, son, I don't know what you're talking about. I bought those designs fair and square, which means I can do whatever I want with them."

That wasn't possible. "Who did you buy them from?"

"You don't think I'm going to give you the name of my designer, do you?" Vernon let out such a loud guffaw that Jasper moved the phone away from his ear again. "You have a lot of gall, son, to claim my designs as your own. A lot of gall. Didn't your daddy teach you anything about this business before he headed to the great beyond?"

"You must not have heard me, Mr. Spears." Jasper did his best to push down the growing pressure against his chest. "*I'm* the designer. Whoever sold you those designs stole them, but they belong to me. You can't manufacture that line."

"Seems to me that you're the one who isn't listening. I *bought* those designs. They're mine. And the first run of that line is already on its way to my distributor in New York City. Even if I believed you came up with those fine designs, it's too late to stop my production. And, son, just so we're clear—I *don't* believe you. Kane Pottery never sold anything like what I'm selling now."

A cackling laugh reverberated against Jasper's ear.

"I'm telling you again, and I'm telling you this for your own good. You might as well close your doors. You may have your daddy's business, but you didn't inherit his sense or his guts."

The slam disconnecting the call reverberated through the line.

Jasper gripped his receiver then set it on the cradle. Those designs, ones he'd created and tweaked over several years, were meant to propel Kane Pottery into a new era. His father had refused to even consider them, but Jasper was certain that, as the Depression eased, demand for new products would rise. As Vernon had said, an optimistic country would be interested in decorative items.

Unfortunately, Vernon decided to give the customers what they wanted with Jasper's ideas.

What to do now?

Jasper pushed away from his desk and stared through the glass to the factory floor below and the beehive of activity occurring there. Most of these employees had been at the company for years. They'd watched Jasper grow up, and now they were counting on him.

Hard to imagine that one of them could have betrayed him.

Vernon had made it clear that he wanted Jasper to fail. Then there would be one less competitor in the Pottery Capital. But Jasper wouldn't go down without a fight. He couldn't stop Vernon from going forward with the stolen designs. But he'd do whatever it took to find out who'd stolen them and make sure it didn't happen again.

He returned to his desk, pulled the latest edition of the *Crooksville News* from a shelf, and flipped through the pages till he found the advertisement he wanted. The P&I Detective Agency based in nearby Zanesville promised professional service and discreet confidentiality.

Exactly what Jasper needed. He picked up his phone.

Roll the stacked sheets—paper, carbon, paper, carbon, paper—into the Underwood typewriter. Type, type, type. Remove the completed report. Separate the pages from the carbons and place them in the appropriate boxes for filing. Repeat.

After all of Polly Matthews's intensive training with the renowned Pinkerton Detective Agency, this was now her life.

She once again questioned the wisdom of joining her brother in opening their own agency. The proposed business arrangement had sounded perfect when he suggested it. After all, he'd been a Pinkerton man for a few years, and Polly had completed her training with impeccable scores.

"Together, we can build the most reputable detective agency in southern Ohio," Isaac had said. A dream he still believed in and, to be fair, one that could still come true.

But Polly had expected to be working cases with him—she'd envisioned sleuthing for clues, sneaking into forbidden places, and

in Peculiar, Missouri

solving crimes in the grand traditions of Edgar Allan Poe's C. Auguste Dupin and Sir Arthur Conan Doyle's Sherlock Holmes. Instead, Isaac did the detective work while she filed reports and balanced their books. She'd told him more than once that if she'd wanted to be a secretary, she'd have finished secretarial school instead of quitting after her first year. But Isaac insisted someone needed to keep them organized. Since he didn't type and his penmanship was too atrocious for him to write in the accounting ledgers, those roles naturally fell to her.

If only she'd stayed with the Pinkertons. The famed agency had the foresight to hire Kate Warne, their first woman detective, in 1856—before the Civil War—and had valued her contributions enough to hire even more women. They recognized, as Isaac apparently did not, that women made excellent detectives.

As Polly rolled another sheet of paper into the typewriter, she imagined the thrilling cases she could be working on right this very minute if she hadn't agreed to Isaac's plans. She might be trailing a counterfeiter or hunting a jewel thief or posing as a femme fatale to gain access into a secret society intent on overthrowing the government.

Isaac would laugh at that last scenario, but during her training, Polly had proved herself adept at transforming herself into either a glamourgal or an insignificant spinster.

Yet here she was, stuck in the P&I Detective Agency's storefront office, typing and filing, filing and typing.

Isaac emerged from the inner office—another bone of contention, at least from Polly's point of view, since she longed for an inner office of her own—and perched on the edge of her desk.

"I just got off the phone with the owner of a pottery company down in Crooksville." He handed her a piece of paper covered with his chicken-scratch handwriting. Polly might be the only person on the globe who could decipher it. "Something about one of his competitors stealing designs for what he called 'artistic pottery.'"

Polly leaned away from the typewriter and studied the paper. *Jasper Kane. Pottery. Who cares?* Beneath the smart-alecky question, twice underlined for emphasis, was a telephone number. If Isaac wanted to grow their partnership into an agency that would someday rival Pinkertons, *he* needed to care about the problems of any potential client.

"What does he mean by artistic pottery?" she asked.

Isaac shrugged. "No idea, and I didn't ask."

"Are you going there this afternoon?" Crooksville was about fifteen miles south of Zanesville, which meant Isaac could be gone for over an hour. Probably two. She'd be alone in the office and could practice her self-defense moves without him around to offer his unsolicited comments.

He picked up her desk calendar and flipped through the pages. The summer months had brought with them a lull in business. Either people committed more crimes in cooler months or potential clients cared less about pursuing the miscreants in their lives when sapped by the heat.

"I'm not going there at all," he said.

"Why not?" Polly demanded. "You know as well as I do that we need every case we can get right now." Even one her brother deemed boring.

"Pottery manufacturing may be an important industry around here, but this sounds like a case of petty rivalry to me. After all, a vase is a vase is a vase. Who's to say who came up with what design?"

"I'll call him and get more details." She picked up the handset and started to dial, but Isaac depressed the button.

"Don't bother with that." He ambled to the front window and peered through the glass. "We might have a client with deep, deep pockets in need of our special investigative skills."

Despite herself, Polly couldn't help but be intrigued. "Who's that?"

"I read about it in the *Chillicothe Gazette* this morning. A woman found an intruder in her home a couple of nights ago. He took off when she confronted him, but he left behind a jar of buttons. Police are stumped."

"That sounds intriguing. When do we leave?"

Isaac's thick brows met in the middle. "Not we. Me."

"But you said '*our* special investigative skills.'"

"I meant *our* as in the agency." Isaac twirled his finger as if to encompass the office then waggled it between him and Polly. "Not *our* as in you and me."

She should have known. He'd never give her a chance to prove herself. Her eyes lit upon the scrap of paper. "What about Jasper Kane? If you don't want me calling him, why did you give me his number?"

"So you could call one of your contacts at Pinkerton and find out if there's anything to this design-stealing business. I mean, how could this Kane even prove that he and this other fella didn't come up with similar ideas at the same time?" Isaac gave an exaggerated shrug as if to say there was no plausible answer. "Call him with whatever you find out and send him an invoice. That's about all we can do, but at least we'll make a little money along the way."

Polly didn't appreciate Isaac's indifference to Mr. Kane's situation, but he was right. Any help they offered was better than none.

Though if Isaac wasn't interested in pursuing the matter, perhaps... butterflies swooshed in her stomach.

"When are you going to Chillicothe?" Polly asked, careful to keep her tone indifferent.

"I'll leave on the early-morning train. You can take care of things around here while I'm gone, can't you? It may be several days before I return."

"You know I can," Polly said, miffed he'd even ask such a question. Though in this case, taking care of things would mean closing the office while she took a trip of her own.

Since Isaac refused to help this Jasper Kane, then Polly would take off her secretarial hat and don a deerstalker's cap.

In the grand tradition of Sherlock Holmes.

A Note from the Editors

We hope you enjoyed another book in the Love's a Mystery series, published by Guideposts. For over seventy-five years Guideposts, a nonprofit organization, has been driven by a vision of a world filled with hope. We aspire to be the voice of a trusted friend, a friend who makes you feel more hopeful and connected.

By making a purchase from Guideposts, you join our community in touching millions of lives, inspiring them to believe that all things are possible through faith, hope, and prayer. Your continued support allows us to provide uplifting resources to those in need. Whether through our online communities, websites, apps, or publications, we strive to inspire our audiences, bring them together, comfort, uplift, entertain, and guide them.

To learn more, please go to guideposts.org.